Object Oriented PHP5
The Object Factory Model

Index

Chapter 1
Introduction to OOD

Object Orientated Design (OOD) Principles;

1. OOD uses abstract objects to model the real world.
2. All objects have properties and methods.
3. An object's properties describe some aspect or property intrinsic to the object.
4. An object's methods enable the object to perform some function.
5. An object is an instance of a class.

OOD uses abstract objects to model the real world.

Obviously the real world is a very complex thing to model and describe using abstract objects. However, if you think of the world as being made up of atoms that have combined to form more complex molecules, which in turn have combined to form more complex compounds, then you can see that by combining simple objects we can form models of more complex objects.

All objects have properties and methods.

If we use objects to model the real world, then we have to be able to describe and define our objects. Following the example of atoms and molecules above, we describe a water molecule as H2O. Meaning water is made of 2 hydrogen atoms and 1 oxygen atom. We can then describe hydrogen as having one electron and a neucleus of 1 proton and 1 neutron. And oxygen as having eight electrons and a neucleus of eight protons and neutrons.

So an abstract atom object would have two properties. The number of electrons and a neucleus containing a number of protons and neutrons.

Atoms also combine to make molecules. Some atoms lose electrons during this process, some gain electrons during this process and some share electrons during this process. The losing, gaining or sharing of electrons is the method an atom uses to form a molecule.

So an abstract atom object would have a method that determines whether the atom gains, loses or shares electrons when it encounters another abstract atom object.

An object's properties describe some aspect or property intrinsic to the object.

If we have a hydrogen atom and an oxygen atom, we have two examples of an atom. We can say that the hydrogen atom and the oxygen atom share a common ancestor that can be described as Atom.

In OOD we would say that the hydrogen and oxygen atoms are derived from the Atom class. We could also say that the Atom class is the class from which all other atoms are derived.

So what would the Atom class look like? It would at least have a neucleus property and an electron property that would not specify a number of protons, neutrons or electrons because as soon as we start specifying numbers, we have to name our Atoms.

So a hydrogen atom is an Atom class that has one electron and one proton and one neutron and is therefore an Atom of type Hydrogen. One electron, one proton and one neutron are properties intrinsic to a Hydrogen atom.

An object's methods enable the object to perform some function.

An Atom class is the class from which all other atoms are derived. One thing an Atom needs to know is when it comes into contact with another Atom. So all Atoms would have to share a method that could detect the presence of other Atoms.

So our Atom base class would need to define an Atom detector method (or function) that all derived Atoms can use. Once our Hydrogen atom has detected another Atom it would need a method to determine whether it lost, gained or shared an electron with the detected Atom.

The loss, gain or sharing of electrons would depend on the Type of the Atom detected. So our method would somehow determine the Atom Type and then decide the fate of it's electron.

An object is an instance of a class.

In OOD we use a class to define our Object but we must instantiate our class to use it as an object. Our PHP class file defines our object and instantiating our object loads it into memory so that it can be used.

All of the properties and methods defined and derived in the PHP class file become encapsulated in the instance of the Object.

There are many OOD resources on the web that provide further information on OOD principles but understanding those outlined above are enough to get started with the Object Factory framework used in this book.

http://en.wikipedia.org/wiki/Object-oriented_design
http://softwaredesign.com/objects.html
http://www.developer.com/lang/article.php/3304881/The-Object-Oriented-Thought-Process.htm

Chapter 2
Objects in a Web Context

Objects are used to model the real world. So, what happens in the real world when someone visits a website? We can say that a person uses a web browser to surf the pages of our website.

From this simple description we can see that our website is made up of at least one web page. So we need a web page object. We also have another object here, one that is usually overlooked, and that is the person doing the surfing. We can call this object the User.

There is another object that is not at first apparent and that is usually described as a session. The person surfing the website establishes a session with the website that resides primarily on the web server. Because session has a specific meaning in website programming and doesn't really describe the interaction between User and Page, I am going to call this object State. The State object determines how the User object interacts with the Page object.

The User, Page and State objects interact with each other to deliver content to the web browser. For example, the user clicks on a link and the State object determines if the User is logged in and therefore able to view the content of the requested Page object.

Let's look a little closer at our objects. The User, State and Page objects must be present in order to deliver content to the web browser. We can therefore say that these three objects constitute the Base Classes that all websites are derived from. This forms the foundation upon which we will build all our websites.

The User class needs to define a user manipulating a web browser to surf our site, but we are not really concerned with describing the person doing the surfing. We don't really need to know what colour their eyes are, for example. However, we will typically be collecting data about the person as they move through our website. If the person supplies our site with an email address, we would want to store that information so that we don't have to continually ask the person to enter their email address.

We have called our User a Base Class and we know that Base Classes are classes from which other classes are derived. However, our User class will not typically be any different between different websites. In other words, a generic User object would generally be sufficient for all our websites in the future. Of course, nobody can see the future so we want to define a User class that can be derived from in case the need to do so arises in the future. This is where OOD differs significantly from the procedural, embedded PHP paradign. Once our objects are defined we will never re-write the code. In other words, we will write code once and use it a thousand times knowing that it will always behave in the defined manner. There is no cut, paste and hack, and therefore, no need for re-testing.

Our State object is going to determine what page the User wants to see and whether the User is allowed to see the requested page. For example, before a User visits our site, we don't have a User. Our State object will actually determine if the User has just entered the website or whether we've seen this User on a previous page, or visit. The State object will also instantiate other objects in order to perform tasks like user logons.

The Page object is a Base Class that all pages on the website will be derived from. This is the most complex object and this is also the area where most errors are going to occur. Therefore we need to establish some rules that all derived classes must follow in order to be considered of Type Page. In OOD, rules take the form of an Interface. If the derived objects conform to the Interface, then they can interact with the Base Class. We will also "program to the interface" which is an agile development technique that enables rapid and stable development of derived objects.

All web pages contain a header section that defines the web standard to which the web page will conform and also contains meta tags that hold definitions of keywords and descriptions that are used by search engines to classify web pages. We do not want to have to change our object's code once we have written it, so we will use constants declared in a data file to hold this information. When we create a new website, we need only change our constants in our data file. We don't touch our Base Classes. Changing a Base Class will affect all of the derived classes.

In this Object Factory Framework, the HTML is optimised to be read by browsers, not by humans, so the HTML code is going to look very messy to most PHP developers. The framework stores the ouput from all objects until the last moment and produces what is similar to a burst transmission that can be seen using a performance monitor. By storing the output until the last moment, the user can be redirected to any page using the PHP header function without the "headers already sent" error occuring. The framework also allows for redirection at the object level which makes the site independand of the URL.

The code examples I will show you are taken from projects that I have written previously and in most cases are actual objects that are used in commercial sites that I have written. I will delete sensitive code for this reason and therefore some functions will be empty. The Object Factory Framework download that accompanies this book contains these objects and many more that will not be shown but you will see references to in the code. I don't typically document most of my objects and comments are kept to a minimum. However, I use verbose names that generally describe what a function does and so most PHP programmers should be able to follow the code fairly easily. In the next chapter I describe the workings of the Object Factory Framework and you will see why comments and documentation are fairly redundant.

So, let's look at our objects.

The User object;

```php
<?php
class User{

        private $userid;
        private $username;
        private $pwd;
        private $firstname;
        private $lastname;
        private $screenname;
        private $email;
        private $timezone;
        private $image;
        private $pagetype;
        private $style;
        private $loggedin;
        private $address1;
        private $address2;
        private $postcode;
        private $phone;
        private $wkphone;
        private $mobile;
        private $fax;
        private $state;
        private $country;
        private $ismember;
        private $ip;
        private $datecreated;
        private $duedate;

        public function get_UserId(){
                return $this->userid;
        }
        public function set_UserId($id){
                $this->userid = $id;
        }
        public function get_Username(){
                return $this->username;
        }
        public function get_Pwd(){
                return $this->pwd;
        }
        public function set_Username($un){
                $this->username = md5($un);
        }
        public function set_Pwd($pw){
                $this->pwd = md5($pw);
        }
        public function set_FirstName($fn){
                $this->firstname = $fn;
```

```php
    }
    public function set_LastName($ln){
        $this->lastname = $ln;
    }
    public function set_Nick($sn){
        $this->screenname = $sn;
    }
    public function set_Email($em){
        $this->email = $em;
    }
    public function set_TZ($tz){
        $this->timezone = $tz;
    }
    public function set_Image($img){
        $this->image = $img;
    }
    public function get_FirstName(){
        return $this->firstname;
    }
    public function get_LastName(){
        return $this->lastname;
    }
    public function get_Nick(){
        return $this->screenname;
    }
    public function get_Email(){
        return $this->email;
    }
    public function get_TZ(){
        return $this->timezone;
    }
    public function get_Image(){
        return $this->image;
    }
    public function get_PageType(){
        return $this->pagetype;
    }
    public function set_PageType($pt){
        $this->pagetype = $pt;
    }
    public function get_Style(){
        return $this->style;
    }
    public function set_Style($sty){
        if(is_array($sty)){
            $this->style = $sty;
        }else{
            $this->style[] = $sty;
        }
    }
    public function isLoggedIn(){
        return $this->loggedin;
    }
```

```php
public function set_LoggedIn($val){
    $this->loggedin = $val;
}
public function set_Address1($ad1){
    $this->address1 = $ad1;
}
public function set_Address2($ad2){
    $this->address2 = $ad2;
}
public function set_Postcode($pc){
    $this->postcode = $pc;
}
public function set_Phone($ph){
    $this->phone = $ph;
}
public function set_WkPhone($wph){
    $this->wkphone = $wph;
}
public function set_Mobile($mb){
    $this->mobile = $mb;
}
public function set_Fax($fx){
    $this->fax = $fx;
}
public function set_State($st){
    $this->state = $st;
}
public function set_Country($ct){
    $this->country = $ct;
}
public function get_Address1(){
    return $this->address1;
}
public function get_Address2(){
    return $this->address2;
}
public function get_Postcode(){
    return $this->postcode;
}
public function get_Phone(){
    return $this->phone;
}
public function get_WkPhone(){
    return $this->wkphone;
}
public function get_Mobile(){
    return $this->mobile;
}
public function get_Fax(){
    return $this->fax;
}
public function get_State(){
    return $this->state;
```

```php
    }
    public function get_Country(){
        return $this->country;
    }
    public function get_Ip(){
        return $this->ip;
    }
    public function get_DateCreated(){
        return $this->datecreated;
    }
    public function set_DateCreated($dc){
        $this->datecreated = $dc;
    }
    public function get_DueDate(){
        return $this->duedate;
    }
    public function set_DueDate($dd){
        $this->duedate = $dd;
    }
    public function set_StarSign($sts){
        $this->starsign = $sts;
    }
    public function get_StarSign(){
        return $this->starsign;
    }

    public function __construct(){
        $this->style[0] = 'misc.css';
        $this->style[1] = 'structure.css';
        $this->style[2] = 'footer.css';
        $this->style[3] = 'menu.css';
        $this->style[4] = 'default.css';
        $this->ip = $this->getRealIpAddr();
    }

    private function getRealIpAddr(){
    if (!empty($_SERVER['HTTP_CLIENT_IP'])){
            $ip = $_SERVER['HTTP_CLIENT_IP'];
    }elseif (!empty($_SERVER['HTTP_X_FORWARDED_FOR'])){
            $ip = $_SERVER['HTTP_X_FORWARDED_FOR'];
    }else{
            $ip = $_SERVER['REMOTE_ADDR'];
    }
    return $ip;
    }

    public function Diagnose($inline = true){
        if($inline){
            $s = '<h3>AlgyZone User Dump</h3>';
            $s .= "<PRE>" . print_r($this, true) . "</PRE>";
            $s .= '<h3>--------AlgyZone User Dump Ends
------------</h3>';
            return $s;
```

```
        }else{
              echo '<h3>AlgyZone User Dump</h3>';
              echo "<PRE>" . print_r($this, true) . "</PRE>";
              echo '<h3>--------AlgyZone User Dump Ends
-----------</h3>';
        }
    }


}
?>
```

Daunting? It needn't be. We start with the typical PHP opening tag and then a class definition `class User{`. The next few lines starting with the keyword `private` are property definitions that describe the properties associated with a typical user. Most actually hold address information. The next several lines starting with `public function get_` or `public function set_` are called Accessor functions and are used to expose the privately declared properties to other objects.

The `public function __construct(){`
```
        $this->style[0] = 'misc.css';
        $this->style[1] = 'structure.css';
        $this->style[2] = 'footer.css';
        $this->style[3] = 'menu.css';
        $this->style[4] = 'default.css';
        $this->ip = $this->getRealIpAddr();
    }
```

is a Constructor (that's a double underscore at the start of the function name) and is automatically run when the object is instantiated. Inside the function we assign several stylesheets to a private array called $style. The last line of the Constructor calls a private function

```
private function getRealIpAddr(){
if (!empty($_SERVER['HTTP_CLIENT_IP'])){
            $ip = $_SERVER['HTTP_CLIENT_IP'];
}elseif (!empty($_SERVER['HTTP_X_FORWARDED_FOR'])){
            $ip = $_SERVER['HTTP_X_FORWARDED_FOR'];
}else{
            $ip = $_SERVER['REMOTE_ADDR'];
}
return $ip;
}
```

Which gets the user's IP address.

The last method
```
public function Diagnose($inline = true){
        if($inline){
```

```php
                $s = '<h3>AlgyZone User Dump</h3>';
                $s .= "<PRE>" . print_r($this, true) . "</PRE>";
                $s .= '<h3>--------AlgyZone User Dump Ends
------------</h3>';
                return $s;
        }else{
                echo '<h3>AlgyZone User Dump</h3>';
                echo "<PRE>" . print_r($this, true) . "</PRE>";
                echo '<h3>--------AlgyZone User Dump Ends
------------</h3>';
        }
    }
}
```

is useful for debugging. It will show you what the current instance of the object holds. Remember, in OOD you write the code once and use it again and again. When using the Object Factory Framework, you will never need to even see this code again.

The State object;

```php
<?php
class State{

    protected $qs;
    protected $sessionid;
    protected $obj;

    public function __construct(){
        $this->qs = explode(QS_DELIMITER, $_SERVER['QUERY_STRING']);
        $this->sessionid = session_id();
        $this->obj = new ObjectFactory();
        if(isset($_POST['submit'])){
            if($_POST['submit'] == 'logon'){
                $reg = $this->obj->Create('GateKeeper');
                $reg->LogonUser(addslashes($_POST['email']),
addslashes($_POST['pwd']));
            }
        }
    }

    public function LoadState($type = 'null', $obj){
        switch(strtolower($type)){
            case 'user':
                return $this->UserState($obj);
                break;
            default:
                return $this->UserState($obj);
                break;
        }
    }

    public function StoreState($type = 'null', $obj){
```

```php
            switch(strtolower($type)){
                case 'user':
                    $this->StoreUserState($obj);
                    break;
                default:
                    $this->StoreUserState($obj);
                    break;
            }
    }

    private function UserState($user){
        $user = $this->CheckUser($user);
        $p = array_pop($this->qs);
        if(strlen($p) == 0){
            $user->set_PageType(START_PAGE);
        }else{
            $user->set_PageType($p);
        }
        $this->StoreState('User', $user);
        return $user;
    }

    private function StoreUserState($obj){
        $_SESSION['User'] = serialize($obj);
    }

    private function CheckUser($user){
        if(!isset($_SESSION['User'])){
            $user = $this->obj->Create('User');
            $user->set_UserId($this->guid());
        }else{
            $user = unserialize($_SESSION['User']);
        }
        return $user;
    }

    protected function guid(){
        if (function_exists('com_create_guid')){
            return com_create_guid();
        }
        mt_srand((double)microtime()*10000);//optional for php 4.2.0 and
up.
        $charid = strtoupper(md5(uniqid(rand(), true)));
        $hyphen = chr(45);// "-"
        $uuid = chr(123)// "{"
        .substr($charid, 0, 8).$hyphen
        .substr($charid, 8, 4).$hyphen
        .substr($charid,12, 4).$hyphen
    .substr($charid,16, 4).$hyphen
    .substr($charid,20,12)
    .chr(125);// "}"
        return $uuid;
    }
```

```php
        protected function DbConn(){
                $conn = mysql_connect(SERVER, STATE_USER, STATE_PWD) or die ('I
cannot connect to the database because: ' . mysql_error());
                mysql_select_db (DATABASE);
                if($conn){
                        return $conn;
                }else{
                        return null;
                }
        }

}
?>
```

The State object is a little more complex than the User object. It has fewer properties and more methods. This is to be expected as the State object could be thought of as a utility object in that it is used to perform certain tasks rather than hold data.

After the class definition `class State{` we see three property declarations;

```php
protected $qs;
protected $sessionid;
protected $obj;
```

These are declared using the `protected` keyword. A `protected` property or method can be accessed by a derived (or child) class but is considered private to the instance of the object. In other words, if you derive a class from State, you will be able to access these properties without re-declaring them in the derived class.

```php
public function __construct(){
        $this->qs = explode(QS_DELIMITER, $_SERVER['QUERY_STRING']);
        $this->sessionid = session_id();
        $this->obj = new ObjectFactory();
        if(isset($_POST['submit'])){
                if($_POST['submit'] == 'logon'){
                        $reg = $this->obj->Create('GateKeeper');
                        $reg->LogonUser(addslashes($_POST['email']),
addslashes($_POST['pwd']));
                }
        }
}
```

The Constructor assigns values to the protected properties and looks for a particular postback event. This is a little complex and needs some explanation.

This line `$this->qs = explode(QS_DELIMITER, $_SERVER['QUERY_STRING']);`

explodes the querystring using a querystring delimiter defined in the data file and assigns the resulting array to the protected property `$qs` . I did this because I was using a / character to give me a nice search engine friendly URL in the site I wrote this for.

This line `$this->sessionid = session_id();` uses the PHP function session_id() to get the current session id or create a new session id as required and assigns it to the protected property `$sessionid` .

This line `$this->obj = new ObjectFactory();` instantiates an Object Factory object and assigns it to the `$obj` protected property.

In the User object, the user's properties were essentially equalivent to variables that any PHP programmer would be familar with. The State object demonstrates that properties can be anything including arrays and other objects.

This part of the Constructor;

```
if(isset($_POST['submit'])){
        if($_POST['submit'] == 'logon'){
                $reg = $this->obj->Create('GateKeeper');
                $reg->LogonUser(addslashes($_POST['email']),
addslashes($_POST['pwd']));
                }
        }
```

looks for a postback event. If it finds one, it looks to see if it is a "logon" event. If it is a "logon" event it uses it's Object Factory to create a GateKeeper object and assigns this object to a local variable `$reg` . It then calls the public function LogonUser passing it two variables.

There are several important concepts to understand here. Any PHP programmer familiar with using PHP objects will have come up against the lazy instantiation issues that usually require the use of autoloaders. With lazy instantiation, objects are not always available at the time they are required and this causes errors to be thrown. The Object Factory Framework stops all that rubbish. The Object Factory builds objects when they are required and so they are always available when you call their methods.

The other concept is the PostBack event. I was really surprised to find several of my colleagues didn't understand that when a form is posted to the web server, it contains the value of all the named elements on the form including the value of the submit button. So I was seeing people name the submit button "logon" and assign it the value "Submit" e.g. <input type="submit" name="logon" value="Submit" /> so if they had several forms on a page they would have to check for each PostBack event and then check for the existance of the form elements expected.

e.g.
if(isset($_POST['logon'])){

```
        if(isset($_POST['username'])){
                .....
        }
    }
```

If you name your submit button "submit" and assign the value of the action the user is performing when they click it e.g. <input type="submit" name="submit" value="logon" /> you only have to check for one PostBack event and then use the value posted to determine the action to take.

The State object contains two public functions;

```php
public function LoadState($type = 'null', $obj){
    switch(strtolower($type)){
        case 'user':
            return $this->UserState($obj);
            break;
        default:
            return $this->UserState($obj);
            break;
    }
}

public function StoreState($type = 'null', $obj){
    switch(strtolower($type)){
        case 'user':
            $this->StoreUserState($obj);
            break;
        default:
            $this->StoreUserState($obj);
            break;
    }
}
```

These two functions define what the State object actually does. Each contains a switch statement that really only performs one function in each case. The LoadState() function returns the User object and the StoreState() function stores the User object.

I put the switch statement in here because if a State object ever needed to do more, then it would be a simple matter of adding a case statement and an associated private function to perform the task. I would suggest that if you wanted to make a State object do more, that you overload these functions to perform the required tasks rather than alter them directly.

The
```php
private function UserState($user){
    $user = $this->CheckUser($user);
    $p = array_pop($this->qs);
    if(strlen($p) == 0){
        $user->set_PageType(START_PAGE);
```

```
        }else{
            $user->set_PageType($p);
        }
        $this->StoreState('User', $user);
        return $user;
    }
```

The first line `$user = $this->CheckUser($user);` calls a private function CheckUser() to make sure we are dealing with the current User object.

`$p = array_pop($this->qs);` assigns the last element in the querystring to a local variable. The following if statement determines if the local variable actually holds any data. If it doesn't, then we assume the User is new to the site and set the User's PageType property to the name of the landing page of our site that we define in our data file. If the local variable does contain data, we assign that value to the User's PageType property. So the last element in the querystring needs to be the name of the Page Type object that the user requests by clicking on a link.

The second last line `$this->StoreState('User', $user);` calls a private function that will store the current state of the User object.

The last line `return $user;` returns our User object to the LoadState() function.

The `private function CheckUser($user){`
```
        if(!isset($_SESSION['User'])){
            $user = $this->obj->Create('User');
            $user->set_UserId($this->guid());
        }else{
            $user = unserialize($_SESSION['User']);
        }
        return $user;
    }
```

Looks to see if we have a current user in session. If not it creates a User object using the Object Factory and gives the new User a unique id. If we have a User in session, it gets the current User object into a usable state by unserializing it.

The `private function StoreUserState($obj){`
```
        $_SESSION['User'] = serialize($obj);
    }
```

Serializes the User object into a session variable.

The `protected function guid()` generates unique ids.

The `protected function DbConn(){` creates a database connection in the standard way.

And that's the State object in a nutshell.

Here's the big one, the Page object. But firstly lets look at the Interface I mentioned above. The Interface contains the rules that all Page Type objects must play by. By convention an Interface is called the same name as it's Base Class prefixed with a lowercase i.

```php
<?php
interface iPage
{
        public function Initialise();
        public function writeContent();
        public function Finalise();
}
?>
```

So we see that a Page object must contain three public functions called Initialise(), writeContent() and Finalise(). Notice also that the functions are simply named and have no function!

OK, here goes...

```php
<?php
class Page{

        protected $user;
        private $script;

        public function get_User(){
                return $this->user;
        }
        public function set_User($u){
                $this->user = $u;
        }

        public function __construct(){
                $this->script[0] = 'modules.js';
        }

        public function Initialise(){
                return $this->writeHeaders(true);
        }

        public function Finalise(){
                return $this->writeFooter(date('Y'), true);
        }
```

```php
	public function onBeforeEvent(){
		return $this->onBeforeContent();
	}

	public function onAfterEvent(){
		return $this->onAfterContent();
	}

	//writes a valid XHTML 1.1 header.
	final protected function writeHeaders($ex){
		session_cache_limiter("must-revalidate");
		$s = '<!DOCTYPE html PUBLIC "-//W3C//DTD XHTML 1.0
Transitional//EN" "http://www.w3.org/TR/xhtml1/DTD/xhtml1-transitional.dtd">'
			. '<html xmlns="http://www.w3.org/1999/xhtml" xml:lang="en-au">'
			. '<head><title>' . $this->get_Title() . '</title><meta http-
equiv="Content-Script-Type" content="text/javascript" /><meta http-
equiv="Content-Type" content="text/html; charset=UTF-8" />'
			. '<meta http-equiv="Content-Style-Type" content="text/css"
/><meta http-equiv="Page-Enter" content="blendtrans(duration=0.15)" />';
		if($this->get_Refresh()){
			$s .= '<meta http-equiv="Refresh" content="' . $this-
>get_Refresh() . '" />';
			}
		$s .= '<meta name="author" content="' . AUTHOR . '" />'
			. '<meta name="generator" content="' . GENERATOR . '" />'
			. '<meta name="robot" content="' . ROBOT . '" /><meta
name="revisit-after" content="' . REVISIT_AFTER . '" />'
			. '<meta name="distribution" content="' . DISTRIBUTION . '"
/><meta name="keywords" content="' . KEYWORDS . '" />'
			. '<meta name="description" content="' . DESCRIPTION . '" /><meta
name="classification" content="' . CLASSIFICATION . '" />'
			. '<meta name="product_category" content="' . PRODUCT_CATEGORY .
'" /><meta name="products" content="' . PRODUCTS . '" />'
			. '<meta name="google-site-verification" content="" /><style
type="text/css">';
		$s .= $this->getStyles();
		$s .= '</style>';
		$s .= $this->getScripts();
		$s .= '</head><body>';
		if($ex){
			$s .= '<table id="content" cellpadding="0"
cellspacing="0"><tr><td>';
			}
		return $s;
	}

	final protected function writeFooter($year, $ex){
		$s = '';
		if($ex){
			$s .= '</td></tr></table>';
		}
		$s .= '<div id="footer">';
```

```php
            $s .= '<span class="copy">Copyright &copy; 2009 - ' . $year;
            $s .= '</span></div>';
            return $s . '</body></html>';
    }

    private function getStyles(){
            $s = '<!--';
            $arr = $this->get_User()->get_Style();
            for($i = 0;$i<count($arr);$i++){
                    $s .= '@import url("' . STYLE_DIRECTORY . $arr[$i] . '");';
            }
            return $s . '//-->';
    }

    private function getScripts(){
            $s = '';
            for($i=0;$i<count($this->script);$i++){
                    $s .= '<script type="text/javascript" src="' .
SCRIPTS_DIRECTORY . $this->script[$i] . '"></script>';
            }
            return $s . $this->writeGoogleAnalytics();
    }

    protected function writeHeading($head, $encaps = false){
            if($encaps){
                    $s = '<div id="header">' . $head . '</div>';
            }else{
                    $s = $head;
            }
            return $s;
    }

    protected function writeMenu(){
            $obj = new ObjectFactory();
            $m = $obj->Create('Menu');
            return $m->writeNav($this->user->get_PageType());
    }

    protected function writeBreadCrumb(){
            $obj = new ObjectFactory();
            $bc = $obj->Create('BreadCrumb');
            return $bc->writeBreadCrumb();
    }

    protected function writeAdSense(){
            $s = '';
            return $s;
    }

    protected function writeGoogleAnalytics(){
            $s = '';
            return $s;
    }
```

```php
    protected function emailToFriends(){
        return '<span id="emailToFriends"><a href="mailto:?body=Check out
this site. ' . DEFAULT_LNK . '">e-mail to friends <img
src="Images/email1.jpg" alt="email icon" title="click to email link to
friend" width="15" height="10" /></a></span>';
    }

    protected function ejectUser(){
        $obj = new ObjectFactory();
        $sm = $obj->Create('SiteManager');
        $pge = $obj->Create(START_PAGE);
        if(!is_object($this->get_User())){
            $this->set_User($obj->Create('User'));
        }
        $this->get_User()->set_PageType(START_PAGE);
        $pge->set_User($this->get_User());
        $sm->Manage($pge);
        die();
    }

    public function Diagnose(){
        echo '<h3>AlgyZone Page Dump</h3>';
        echo "<PRE>" . print_r($_SERVER, true) . "</PRE>";
        echo '<h3>--------AlgyZone Page Dump Ends ------------</h3>';
    }

}
?>
```

The Page object is the base class all pages on our website are derived from. Therefore we want our base class to perform all of the functions common to all pages on any site. Looking through the code we see that most of the methods build a HTML string. This is important to understand if you are used to building web pages in the traditional embedded PHP within HTML method. All HTML must be escaped correctly when using the Object Factory Model or you will get errors. One way to do this is to use a WYSIWYG editor to produce your page and lift the HTML into your function.

OK, let's walk through the Page object.

After the class definition `class Page{` we declare two properties, one protected and one private.

```php
    protected $user;
    private $script;
```

Our $user property will hold our User object so that we can expose our User properties to the pages of our web site.

The $script property is an array that holds links to our javascript files.

Next we have two Accessor functions for our User object;

```
public function get_User(){
    return $this->user;
}
public function set_User($u){
    $this->user = $u;
}
```

We then come to our constructor;

```
public function __construct(){
    $this->script[0] = 'modules.js';
}
```

This is assigning a modules.js file to the first element in the $script array. Because $script has no Accessor functions and is declared private, it is readonly. That is, it is only available to the Page base class. If you have other javascript files, then you will need to customise this constructor to suit your needs.

Now we have the meat of the Page class.

```
public function Initialise(){
    return $this->writeHeaders(true);
}

public function Finalise(){
    return $this->writeFooter(date('Y'), true);
}
```

These two functions set the web pages up. They produce the opening HTML tags (in the Initialise function) and the closing HTML tags (in the Finalise function). This means that every Page Type object derived from this base class will automatically write all the HTML required down to, and including, the <body> tag and automatically write all the closing tags after, and including, the </body> tag.

Effectively, all you, as a web developer, have to worry about is the content required for any given page.

```
public function onBeforeEvent(){
    return $this->onBeforeContent();
}

public function onAfterEvent(){
    return $this->onAfterContent();
```

}

The two public functions above are used to perform tasks that may be required before the page loads or after the page loads, respectively. This is a mechanism that I put in incase changes are required after the website has published. These two functions can be called by the Object Factory Framework to perform tasks that were not forseen at design time.

The `final protected function writeHeaders($ex){` is called by the Initialise function as seen above. The final keyword simply means no changes will be made to the function. The $ex parameter (boolean) will insert a one cell table after the <body> tag if set to true.

The `final protected function writeFooter($year, $ex){` is called by the Finalise function as seen above. It takes two parameters. $year is displayed in the copyright information and $ex should be the same (either true or false) as passed to the Initialise function. You may want to customise this function as regards the copyright message.

We then have two private methods; `private function getStyles(){` and `private function getScripts(){` These two methods are called by the Initialise function and are used to build links to CSS style sheets and any Javascript files that are required.

The `protected function` writeHeading($head, $encaps = `false`){ is a method that derived classes can access and is used to write a heading for a page. The $head parameter is the heading to be displayed and the $encaps parameter will encapsulate the $head string in a <div> tag.

All pages on a website require navigation and this function;

```
protected function writeMenu(){
    $obj = new ObjectFactory();
    $m = $obj->Create('Menu');
    return $m->writeNav($this->user->get_PageType());
}
```

will keep the navigation consistant across the site. As you can see it asks the Object Factory to create a menu object and passes the current page type as requested by the User to a Menu method called writeNav. By passing the current page type we can make our menu context sensitive.

The `protected function` writeBreadCrumb(){
```
    $obj = new ObjectFactory();
    $bc = $obj->Create('BreadCrumb');
    return $bc->writeBreadCrumb();
}
```

behaves in the same way as the menu object but produces a breadcrumb navigation bar.

The `protected function writeAdSense(){` is one of those sensitive functions mentioned above and has had the content striped for privacy reasons. You will need to cut and paste your own google adsense string into this function.

The `protected function writeGoogleAnalytics()` is again a sensitive function and will need to be customised to your requirements using cut and paste. It is called by the getScripts() function when the page headers are being built.

The `protected function emailToFriends(){` will write a little mailto link for any page that calls it. Handy for your viral marketing campaign. You may want to customise the output a little as regards the <img /> tag.

The protected function `ejectUser(){` is an example of object level redirection. I will talk about this later as what is hapening here will become clearer after I have shown you the Object Factory framework in the next chapter. You would use this function to direct a user to a start page for your site if you didn't want users to access material before registering, for example.

The `public function Diagnose(){` dumps the contents of the $_SERVER array to the browser and is useful when debugging.

The User, State and Page objects combine to describe every web page on every website on the web today. Do not be daunted by these objects. If you decide to customise the functions mentioned above, that is the last time you will need to see the User or Page objects.

Once an object is written, you will typically never look at the code again. This is one of the reasons why the Object Factory Model is so beneficial to creating PHP websites. You write the code once, test it to aproval stage and then re-use the code again and again without actually looking at the code.

Chapter 3
The Object Factory Framework

This framework came about in response to some design criteria associated with a contract I took on to develop an online hardware store. I was told at the initial meeting that I would be able to start the project from scratch and the overriding criteria was for the company to be able to "pump out more stores" easily.

My background is actually as a Senior Developer in the .NET world creating WinForm and Windows Service applications using C# so I tend to think Object Orientatedly.

I have been developing websites commercially since 1996 and at the time PHP first came out I was using VBScript 5.6 as a scripting language behind my sites. I looked at PHP 1.x and thought it was a load of crap. It was not until PHP 4.x came out that I started to take it seriously again. Now we have PHP 5.x and a nice stable object model so all is well with the world again.

When I started the hardware store contract there was a slight delay as members of the team were away on vacation. I was directed to work with another contractor on a project using CakePHP. I spent the first two days helping him design the database he would later use. CakePHP is a Model View Control framework and is very good at what it does.

I don't like MVC for several reasons. Firstly, although it is robust and stable, when you apply it to the context of most websites it is totally over engineered. Most commercial websites consist of 5 – 10 pages. They can usually be built using a WYSIWYG editor and reside as static HTML pages on a webserver.

Secondly, when using MVC you have to design and build your database first. I don't like to do things this way. I like to build my database as I go, rather than having to spend hours trying to figure out what might be required. Especially if the project design specifications have not been finalised.

Thirdly, MVC tends to be quite expensive in terms of server resources. The MVC pages tend to load slowly at the start and interactions with the database tend to be over the top. It can take hundreds of hits to the database to make a simple update to a single table.

If you have a site like FaceBook in mind, then you should probably look at MVC. If you want something with a tiny server foot print and is lightening fast, there are alternatives.

So I got to thinking, what if I could develop something that would drive my objects so that when the sites needed to be pumped out, all the developers needed to think about was the content to put in front of the users?

I started to build the Object Factory Model. At the end of the first week there was a progress meeting. I had to show the managers what progress I had made. Of course, the OFM framework is invisible to users and the managers wouldn't know what they were looking at if I showed them the code.

Thursday came around and the framework was nearly complete, so I cobbled together some very basic pages based loosely on some example sites my supervisor had shown me. I showed this to the managers at the Friday meeting and on Monday morning my supervisor sat down with me and threw the last weeks work in the recycle bin.

It is actually very fortunate that he did because now the OFM is my intellectual property and I can share it with you readers. It is too good to have just one company use it.

In order to use the Object Factory Framework it is necessary to understand that we are no longer building web pages in the traditional sense. We will now be building objects of type web page.

Most web sites consist of several individual web pages linked together through hyperlinks in a menu or site navigation. A typical website will have a landing, or home page, an "about" page, a contact page and perhaps several "product" pages. These will all reside in the root folder and each page would need to be updated as changes were required.

As the user navigates through the site, each page is published to the web browser as required.

Some scripted sites use a recursive design model that calls up the content displayed on the page as required but usually becomes hellish to maintain as this tends to create elaborate code paths to functions that ususally sit on a "utils" page somewhere.

What if we could have a framework that was infinately scaleable and yet robust so that changes could be made easily without affecting other parts of the site. Oh, and changes must always be backward compatable. It must have a tiny server footprint and still deliver outstanding download speed. It should be easy enough to use that our development team can take to it like a fish to water. We also want to be able to write something once and use it forever.

Enter the The Object Factory Model Framework.

The OFMF uses a recursive design model. All links within the site need to be relative. It takes 180 Kb of file space or less on a server.

Name	Date modified	Type	Size
Css	11/03/2011 5:49 PM	File folder	
Images	11/03/2011 5:49 PM	File folder	
Objects	11/03/2011 5:49 PM	File folder	
Scripts	11/03/2011 5:49 PM	File folder	
data.php	15/10/2010 10:03 ...	PHP File	2 KB
dbadata.php	23/11/2010 9:50 AM	PHP File	1 KB
includes.php	10/10/2010 1:27 PM	PHP File	1 KB
index.php	17/10/2010 9:57 AM	PHP File	1 KB

Image 1. Typical file structure at the root directory

The image above shows the typical install of the OFMF. It is not necessary to maintain this structure but making changes will require you to teach your ObjectFactory object the new locations to find files.

So lets jump right in with what is happening here. We have four folders and four files in our root directory. The folders contain exactly what you'd expect from their names.

The data.php file;

```php
<?php
define('AUTHOR', 'Alister Rutledge - AlgyZone Pty Ltd - www.AlgyZone.com');
define('GENERATOR', 'hand crafted');
define('ROBOT', 'index,follow');
define('REVISIT_AFTER', '7 days');
define('DISTRIBUTION', 'Global');
define('KEYWORDS', '');
define('DESCRIPTION', '');
define('CLASSIFICATION', '');
define('PRODUCTS', '');
define('PRODUCT_CATEGORY', '');
define('INDEX_TITLE', '');
define('UPLOAD_TITLE', '');
define('CONTACT_TITLE', '');
define('ERROR_TITLE', 'Error');
define('STYLE_DIRECTORY', 'Css/');
define('SCRIPT_DIRECTORY', 'Scripts/');

define('QS_DELIMITER', '/');
define('START_PAGE', 'Index');

// Date formats
define('MYSQL_DATETIME', 'Y-m-d H:i:s');
define('MYSQL_YEAR', 'Y');
define('MYSQL_MONTH', 'm');
```

```php
define('MYSQL_DAY', 'd');
define('LONG_DATETIME', 'jS F Y g i s');
define('LONG_DATE', 'jS F Y');
define('SHORT_DATE', 'jS M Y');

define('SITE_HEADING', '<h1></h1>');
define('HOME_HEADING', '');

define('SECURE_LNK', '');
define('DEFAULT_LNK', '');

define('LOST_PWD_MESSAGE', 'A new password is ; ');
define('MAILTO_ADDRESS', '');
?>
```

defines all the constants used throughout the framework and new constants should be added here as required. One of the main diciplines to follow is to keep similar things in one place.

The dbdata.php file;

```php
<?php
//dbconn
define('SERVER', '');
define('USER', '');
define('PWD', '');
define('STATE_USER', '');
define('STATE_PWD', '');
define('DATABASE', '');
?>
```

defines all the database constants. I have separated these from the data.php file as these constants are typically different between development and deployment. By separating them, we limit the number of deployment errors we generate.

The includes.php file;

```php
<?php
session_start();
require_once 'dbadata.php';
require_once 'data.php';
require_once 'Objects/ObjectFactory.php';
require_once 'Objects/BaseClasses/IPage.php';
require_once 'Objects/BaseClasses/Page.php';
?>
```

starts a session if one hasn't already been started using the standard PHP function session_start(). It then uses the require_once directive to load five files. The first two are the data files oulined above. The last three are the ObjectFactory, the Page object interface and the

Page object. If you change where these files reside, you will need to change these file paths.

The index.php file;

```php
<?php
require_once 'includes.php';
$obj = new ObjectFactory();
$state = $obj->Create('State');
$user = $obj->Create('User');
$user = $state->LoadState('User', $user);
$router = $obj->Create('Router');
$router->Route($user);
$state->StoreState('User', $user);
unset($obj);
unset($user);
unset($state);
unset($router);
?>
```

is the engine that drives the entire framework. It is important to understand that we call this file recursively at every web request.

The first line uses the require_once directive to load the includes.php file. Then an ObjectFactory object is created and assigned to the variable $obj. Next a State object is created and assigned to the $state variable. Then a User object is created and assigned to the $user variable.

We have used our ObjectFactory to create the two objects that exist at this time in the real world. State and User as outlined in Chapter 2.

We then call the LoadState() method of our State object to return the current User. Next we create a Router object using the ObjectFactory and assign it to the variable $router. We then ask the Router to route our User.

Our State object is then directed to store the current state of our User. It is interesting to understand that by the time this method is called, our page has been sent to the user's browser.

Lastly, we use the unset() PHP function to destroy all our objects and thereby release all resources back to the server.

Typically you, as a developer, will never look at this file again.

We have a mystery object here, the Router object. Let's have a closer look;

```php
<?php
class Router{
```

```
    protected $obj;
    protected $sm;

    public function __construct(){
        $this->obj = new ObjectFactory();
        $this->sm = $this->obj->Create('SiteManager');
    }

    public function Route($user, $type = 'null'){
        $page = $this->obj->Create($user->get_PageType());
        $page->set_User($user);
        $this->Manage($page, $type);
        //$page->Diagnose();
    }

    private function Manage($page, $type){
        $this->sm->Manage($page, $type);
    }

}
?>
```

After the class definition `class Router{` we declare two protected properties. There are no Accessor functions for these properties, $obj and $sm, so they are not exposed to other objects but may be overloaded in a derived class.

In the
```
public function __construct(){
    $this->obj = new ObjectFactory();
    $this->sm = $this->obj->Create('SiteManager');
}
```

constructor we see that $obj is an ObjectFactory and in the next line we see that $obj is used to create a SiteManager object. Remember that the constructor is always executed when the object is instantiated. This means that the SiteManager object will always be ready to be used when required. No autoloading classes.

In the
```
public function Route($user, $type = 'null'){
    $page = $this->obj->Create($user->get_PageType());
    $page->set_User($user);
    $this->Manage($page, $type);
    //$page->Diagnose();
}
```

which is called on the index.php page on line seven, we set a local variable $page to a Page of Type requested by the User. We get the Page Type that the User requests from the State object.

Next we call the set_User() Accessor from the Page object just created passing it the User that the Router has been asked to route. This will expose all the User's properties to the Page object.

`$this->Manage($page);` calls the private function Manage() passing it the newly created Page of Type requested by the User.

The last line of the Route() function is commented out. Uncomment this line during debugging to dump the $_SERVER data associated with the newly created Page.

The
```php
private function Manage($page, $type){
    $this->sm->Manage($page, $type);
}
```

Uses the SiteManager created in the constructor to manage the Page of Type requested by the User.

Let's have a look at the SiteManager object;

```php
<?php
class SiteManager{

    protected $pub;

    public function __construct(){
        $obj = new ObjectFactory();
        $this->pub = $obj->Create('Publisher');
    }

    public function Manage($page, $type = 'null'){
        switch(strtolower($type)){
            case'std':
            case'stand':
            case'standard':
                $this->pub->Store($this->Standard($page));
            break;
            case'bfr':
            case'before':
                $this->pub->Store($this->Before($page));
            break;
            case'aft':
            case'after':
                $this->pub->Store($this->After($page));
            break;
            case'bfraft':
            case'brat':
            case'bfat':
            case'beforeafter':
                $this->pub->Store($this->BeforeAfter($page));
```

```php
                break;
            default:
                    $this->pub->Store($this->Standard($page));
                break;
        }
        $this->pub->Publish();
    }

    private function Standard($page){
        $s = $page->Initialise();
        $s .= $page->writeContent();
        $s .= $page->Finalise();
        return $s;
    }

    private function Before($page){
        $s = $page->Initialise();
        $s .= $page->onBeforeEvent();
        $s .= $page->writeContent();
        $s .= $page->Finalise();
        return $s;
    }

    private function After($page){
        $s = $page->Initialise();
        $s .= $page->writeContent();
        $s .= $page->onAfterEvent();
        $s .= $page->Finalise();
        return $s;
    }

    private function BeforeAfter($page){
        $s = $page->Initialise();
        $s .= $page->onBeforeEvent();
        $s .= $page->writeContent();
        $s .= $page->onAfterEvent();
        $s .= $page->Finalise();
        return $s;
    }

}
?>
```

After the declaration class SiteManager{ We find a protected variable $pub. In the constructor we see that $pub is a Publisher object. The public function Manage($page, $type = 'null'){ has a switch(strtolower($type)){ statement that calls one of several private functions, each of which will call combinations of methods of the $page object and return a string. The local Publisher object $pub is asked to store the returned string and is asked to

```php
$this->pub->Publish();
```

directly after the switch statement.

The Publisher Class looks like;

```php
<?php
class Publisher{
    private $str;

    public function __construct(){

    }

    public function Store($strg){
        try{
            $this->str .= $strg;
        }catch (Exception $e) {
        return false;
        }
      return true;
    }
    public function Publish(){
        print(stripslashes($this->str));
        flush();
    }
}
?>
```

The `public function Store($strg){` builds a string and `public function Publish(){` prints the string to the browser.

The only object left is the Object Factory, so here it is;

```php
<?php
class ObjectFactory{
    public function __construct(){

    }

    public function Create($type)
    {
        if (@include_once 'Objects/' . $this->BaseClass($type) . '.php') {
            return new $type;
        } else {
            $this->OFError('Object not found');
            //throw new Exception ('Object not found');
        }
    }
```

```php
private function BaseClass($type){
    switch($type){
        case 'User':
        case 'Router':
        case 'Page':
        case 'State':
        case 'SiteManager':
        case 'Publisher':
        case 'Menu':
        case 'Validator':
        case 'PostMaster':
        case 'Error':
        case 'BreadCrumb':
        case 'KeyMaster':
        case 'GateKeeper':
        case 'DbAdmin':
        case 'Payment':
        case 'MakePayment':
        case 'ConfirmPayment':
        case 'ProcessPayment':
        case 'Logout':
        case 'Receipt':
        case 'AccountExpired':
        case 'FileUploader':
        case 'MediaPlayer':
        case 'Paginator':
            return 'BaseClasses/' . $type;
            break;
        case 'LogonForm':
        case 'RegistrationForm':
        case 'ContactForm':
        case 'PaymentForm':
        case 'ConfirmPaymentForm':
        case 'ProfileForm':
        case 'UpdateProfileForm':
        case 'CreateAccountForm':
        case 'FeedBackForm':
            return 'Forms/' . $type;
            break;
        case 'ContactDetails':
        case 'Deliveries':
        case 'PrivacyPolicy':
        case 'RefundsAndReturns':
        case 'TermsAndConditions':
        case 'TermsOfUse':
            return 'Policies/' . $type;
            break;
        case 'Chats':
            return 'Chatroom/' . $type;
            break;
        default:
            return $type;
            break;
```

```
            }
    }

    private function OFError($msg){
        $obj = new ObjectFactory();
        $sm = $obj->Create('SiteManager');
        $pge = $obj->Create('Error');
        $user = $obj->Create('User');
        $pge->set_Message($msg);
        $user->set_PageType('Error');
        $pge->set_User($user);
        $sm->Manage($pge);
        die();
    }

}
?>
```

It looks very simple and it is. Don't think it isn't powerful.

After the class declaration `class ObjectFactory{` we find a public constructor. Then we have the `public function Create($type)` where $type is the name of the object we want to create.

This part of the if statement

```
if (include_once 'Objects/' . $this->BaseClass($type) . '.php') {
    return new $type;
}
```

says if you can find a PHP file called $type.php then return me a new instance of an object of type $type.

This part of the if statement

```
else {
    $this->OFError('Object not found');
    //throw new Exception ('Object not found');
}
```

says if you can't find the PHP file called $type.php then handle the exception.

This part of the code `$this->BaseClass($type)` calls the `private function BaseClass($type){` which returns a path to the requested file. This switch statement needs to be updated when adding new objects to the framework if they don't reside in the Objects folder.

Chapter 4
Self Validating Forms

Writing forms is one area of web design that takes a lot of time and often means re-writing the same or similar code again and again. What if you could just write a form once and plug it into pages as required?

There are two immediate problems to over come. Firstly, a form takes input from a user so the input must be validated and sanitised before it can be stored or used. Secondly, the form's action parameter determines where the user input goes and therefore what subsequent processing occurs.

The first problem can be solved by creating a validation object that can be called anywhere in the website. All validation then becomes standardised and although different senarios require different validation, the validation object can grow over time to handle the new senarios. Any validation already written can be re-used accross all websites.

The second problem can be solved for most instances by leaving the action parameter value blank. The standard action of a form is to call the page it is hosted on. Therefore, by leaving the action parameter blank, we can plug our forms in as needed without changing any code.

There are certain instances where we have to have a value in the action parameter. Logon forms are an example of this. Most of the time a logon will require a secure (https) connection. This will be unique to each website.

A self validating form would be able to validate the user input and inform the user of any mistakes via error messages. It would need to know how to perform it's specific task autonomously so that we could plug it into any page with three lines of code.

Two common forms found on most websites are a contact form and a logon form. These forms have different requirements. For instance, a logon form requires a registration form and a lost password form. A contact form should be able to send an email if the user input is valid.

Let's have a look at a self validating contact form;

```php
<?php
class ContactForm{

    protected $err;
    protected $sent;

    public function __construct(){
```

```php
                $this->err['email'] = false;
                $this->err['comment'] = false;
                $this->sent = 'pending';
                if(isset($_POST['submit'])){
                        if(addslashes($_POST['submit']) == 'Send'){
                                $obj = new ObjectFactory();
                                $v = $obj->Create('Validator');
                                if(!$v->isValid('email',
addslashes($_POST['email']))){
                                        $this->err['email'] = true;
                                }
                                if(!$v->isValid('fname',
addslashes($_POST['comment']))){
                                        $this->err['comment'] = true;
                                }
                                if(!$this->err['email'] && !$this->err['comment']){
                                        $pm = $obj->Create('PostMaster');
                                        $pm->set_Address(CONTACT_ADDRESS);
                                        $pm->set_Subject('Contact from web site');
                                        $pm-
>set_Message(addslashes($_POST['comment']));
                                        $pm->set_From(addslashes($_POST['email']));
                                        if($pm->sendMail()){
                                                $this->sent = 'successful';
                                        }else{
                                                $this->sent = 'failed';
                                        }
                                }
                        }
                }
        }

        public function writeForm(){
                $s = '<form id="contact" method="post" action="">
                <table summary="layout">
                <tr><td class="label">Your Email</td><td><input type="text"
name="email" value="';
                if(isset($_POST['email'])){
                        $s .= $_POST['email'];
                }
                $s .= '" /></td><td class="error">';
                if($this->err['email']){
                        $s .= 'Please enter a valid email address.';
                }
                $s .= '</td><td></td><td></td></tr>
                <tr><td class="label" style="vertical-align:
top;">Comment</td><td colspan="3"><textarea name="comment" cols="50"
rows="10">';
                if(isset($_POST['comment'])){
                        $s .= $_POST['comment'];
                }
                $s .= '</textarea></td><td class="error">';
                if($this->err['comment']){
```

```
                    $s .= 'No comment entered.';
                }
                $s .= '</td></tr>
                <tr><td></td><td><input type="submit" name="submit"
value="Send" /></td><td></td><td></td><td></td></tr>
                </table></form>';
                if($this->sent == 'successful'){
                    $s .= '<p>Your message was successfully sent.</p>';
                }
                if($this->sent == 'failed'){
                    $s .= '<p>An error occurred. Your message was not
sent.</p>';
                }
            return $s;
        }

}
?>
```

After the class declaration `class ContactForm{` we have two protected local variables. In the constructor `public function __construct(){` we find that $err is an array that has two members, email and comment, both initially set to false. We also see that $sent is set to pending.

Then we look for the postback event `if(isset($_POST['submit'])){` We then look to see if the postback event is one related to the contact form `if(addslashes($_POST['submit']) == 'Send'){` . Usually a contact page would only host one form. If more than one form is being hosted the value of the submit button would need to be more specific.

If the postback is our event, we request a Validator object from the Object Factory

```
$obj = new ObjectFactory();
$v = $obj->Create('Validator');
```

The validator then checks the validity of the user input.

If the user input is valid `if(!$this->err['email'] && !$this->err['comment'])` { we request a PostMaster Object from the Object Factory and use it to send the email.

```
$pm = $obj->Create('PostMaster');
$pm->set_Address(CONTACT_ADDRESS);
$pm->set_Subject('Contact from web site');
$pm->set_Message(addslashes($_POST['comment']));
$pm->set_From(addslashes($_POST['email']));
if($pm->sendMail()){
    $this->sent = 'successful';
}else{
```

```
            $this->sent = 'failed';
    }
```

We set the $sent parameter to success or fail accordingly. All this happens as the contact form instantiates.

Our ContactForm has one method `public function writeForm(){` that will write a contact form on a page.

In this line `$s = '<form id="contact" method="post" action="">` we see that the value of the action parameter is blank. The reason the action parameter is included is to comply with our DTD declaration in the page headers.

This line
```
<input type="text" name="email" value="';
        if(isset($_POST['email'])){
                $s .= $_POST['email'];
        }
        $s .= '" />
```

makes our form sticky. It will also provide feed back to our user.

Here our form checks the $err array

```
<td class="error">';
        if($this->err['email']){
                $s .= 'Please enter a valid email address.';
        }
        $s .= '</td>
```

and informs the user of an email address error.

This block of code informs the user of success or failure to send the contact email.
```
if($this->sent == 'successful'){
        $s .= '<p>Your message was successfully sent.</p>';
}
if($this->sent == 'failed'){
        $s .= '<p>An error occurred. Your message was not sent.</p>';
}
```

So here we have a ContactForm object that will work on any web page in the future. We have written it once and there will usually not be a need to alter the code.

To plug it into a page we write;

```
$obj = new ObjectFactory();
$frm = $obj->Create('ContactForm');
```

```php
$s .= $frm->writeForm();
```

Logon forms can have several configurations on a web page. They would usually have username and password fields and a submit button, but they can be displayed as a band across the top of the page. As a postage stamp or a flag on either side of the page. A registered user can logon, so a registration form is required. Also users forget passwords, so a link to a LostPassword object is required.

The logon process typically occurs as a database interaction and would be handled by the State object that we saw in chapter 2. In the case of a successful logon the user would not have the logon form displayed to them again.

```php
<?php
class LogonForm{

    protected $err;

    public function __construct(){
        $this->err['email'] = false;
        $this->err['pwd'] = false;
        if(isset($_POST['submit'])){
            if(addslashes($_POST['submit']) == 'logon'){
                $obj = new ObjectFactory();
                $v = $obj->Create('Validator');
                if(!$v->isValid('email',
addslashes($_POST['email']))){
                    $this->err['email'] = true;
                }
                if(!$v->isValid('pwd', addslashes($_POST['pwd']))){
                    $this->err['pwd'] = true;
                }
            }
        }
    }

    public function writeForm($type = 'null'){
        switch(strtolower($type)){
        case 'flat':
            return $this->writeNormalForm();
            break;
        case 'horiz':
            return $this->writeHorizForm();
            break;
        case 'thin':
        case 'skinny':
            return $this->writeSkinnyForm();
            break;
        default:
            return $this->writeNormalForm();
            break;
        }
```

```php
	}

	private function writeNormalForm(){
		$s = '<form id="logonform" method="post" action="' .
SECURE_LNK .'">
		<table summary="layout">
		<tr><td class="label">Email</td><td><input type="text"
name="email" /></td><td class="error">';
		if($this->err['email']){
			$s .= 'Please enter your email address.';
		}
		$s .= '</td></tr>
		<tr><td class="label">Password</td><td><input type="password"
name="pwd" /></td><td class="error">';
		if($this->err['pwd']){
			$s .= 'Please enter a password.';
		}
		$s .= '</td></tr>
		<tr><td></td><td><input type="submit" name="submit" value="logon"
/></td><td></td></tr>
		<tr><td></td><td colspan="2"><a href="?LostAdminPwd">forgot
password</a></td></tr>
		</table></form>';
		return $s;
	}

	private function writeHorizForm(){
		$s = '<form id="logonform" method="post" action="' .
SECURE_LNK .'">
		<table summary="layout" style="display: inline;">
		<tr><td class="label">Email</td><td><input type="text"
name="email" /></td><td class="label">Password</td><td><input type="password"
name="pwd" /></td><td><input type="submit" name="submit" value="logon"
/></td></tr>
		<tr><td></td><td class="error">';
		if($this->err['email']){
			$s .= 'Please enter your email address.';
		}
		$s .= '</td><td></td><td class="error">';
		if($this->err['pwd']){
			$s .= 'Please enter a password.';
		}
		$s .= '</td><td></td></tr>
		</table></form>';
		return $s;
	}

	private function writeSkinnyForm(){
		$s = '<form id="logonform" method="post" action="' .
SECURE_LNK .'">
		<table summary="layout">
		<tr><td class="label">Email</td></tr>
		<tr><td><input type="text" name="email" /></td></tr>
```

```
            <tr><td class="label">Password</td></tr>
            <tr><td><input type="password" name="pwd" /></td></tr>
            <tr><td><input type="submit" name="submit" value="logon"
/></td></tr>
            <tr><td class="error">';
            if($this->err['email']){
                    $s .= 'Please enter your email address.';
            }
            if($this->err['pwd']){
                    $s .= 'Please enter a password.';
            }
            $s .= '</td></tr>
            <tr><td><a href="?LostPwd">forgot password</a></td></tr>
            </table></form>';
            return $s;
        }


}
?>
```

The LogonForm is similar to the ContactForm and performs self validation in it's constructor. This code won't run if the logon is successful.

After the constructor we find `public function writeForm($type = 'null'){` This is the only public function. It takes a $type optional parameter. We only need to remember one function name writeForm() and pass it a $type if we require a particular layout.

Inside the writeForm() function we have a switch statement `switch(strtolower($type)){` that switches on $type. The the case of $type == flat

```
    case 'flat':
            return $this->writeNormalForm();
            break;
```

return the output of `private function writeNormalForm(){` Which writes a form similar to a ContactForm.

WriteNormalForm() has the line

```
$s = '<form id="logonform" method="post" action="' . SECURE_LNK .'">
```

The action parameter has the value SECURE_LNK which would be a constant defined as a fully qualified URL to the HTTPS protocol in the data.php file. The rest of the form is constructed in much the same way as the ContactForm.

The last row of the table contains a link to a LostPwd object.

```html
<a href="?LostPwd">forgot password</a>
```

The href parameter value is an example of a relative path using the ObjectFactory model. The default behaviour of a web server is to call the default page unless a page is requested. The Apache web server we are using has a default page called index.php. On IIS it would typically be called default.php.

So we don't need to include http://www.somedomain.com/index.php in the URL as that is the default action of the Apache web server.

We saw in Chapter 3 that index.php ran the following code

```php
<?php
require_once 'includes.php';
$obj = new ObjectFactory();
$state = $obj->Create('State');
$user = $obj->Create('User');
$user = $state->LoadState('User', $user);
$router = $obj->Create('Router');
$router->Route($user);
$state->StoreState('User', $user);
unset($obj);
unset($user);
unset($state);
unset($router);
?>
```

In Chapter 2 we saw this line of code in the State object

```php
$p = array_pop($this->qs);
```

That is the State object looking for the last element in an array, in this case the array is the QueryString held locally in the State object. The $_SERVER['QUERY_STRING'] contains everything after the ? in any URL so, as we are always going to call index.php, we don't need to write http://www.somedomain.com/index.php?page=SomeObject in an anchor element. Our href attribute value can simply be ?AnyObject.

It is possible for a person to construct a fully qualified URL to any object in the Object Factory Model. For instance, it is possible to enter http://www.somedomain.com/Objects/Forms/LogonForm.php in the address bar. No error will be thrown but the server returns no output as LogonForm.php won't instantiate without the frame work. If the person enters http://www.myamglam.com/index.php?LogonForm in the address bar, an error is thrown.

Chapter 5
Persistant Objects

The nature of the web is asynchronous. It works like a stimulus/response nervous system. The browser stimulates the server with a request. The server responds with a response. There have, are and will be more, attempts to make the web synchronous. I believe this is wrong. It's great just the way it is.

The Object Factory Framework discussed in this book is a series of objects held in RAM memory for the time it takes the server to respond to the browser request. The server dishes up index.php every time the browser makes a request, as it is never told to serve any other page. All of our pages are Objects of Type Page.

Every time the browser makes a request, the ObjectFactory object looks for the existance of a php file of the Type it is passed as a parameter. If it finds one, it parses it through it's PHP interpreter and then instantiates the requested object in memory.

During the response building process, various methods and properties are exercised which uses RAM and CPU cycles. Both the fastest data processing areas in any computer.

Once the Page object has been published, all the objects are unset and collected by the garbage collector.

We end up with a very fast response and a burst transmission of browser optimised HTML code to the user and nothing left at the server. If we have collected a lot of information on our user, we want to be able to re-use it without the user entering the data again.

The User object only exists in RAM. We need to be able store it between requests and between visits. In order to store an object, we have to be able to represent it as a string. An object represents a structure of data. We use the serialize() function to flatten it into a string. http://php.net/manual/en/function.serialize.php We use unserialize() to return it to an object.

PHP as of 5.2.13 has a problem serializing and unserializing arrays. If the arrays differ in length, index out of bound errors are thrown. One work around is to build your arrays on the fly. Another is to use objects instead of arrays where you can.

So serialize() allows us to physically represent our object. How do we store our serialzed object? One way is to assign it to a $_SESSION['variable']. This will work well if you are not on a load balanced server farm. Another is to write it to a text file. I used to laugh at this suggestion myself until I worked at an online gaming development house. They used text files for internationalisation and it worked just fine. I don't personally use text files as I believe that you will eventually experience file locks.

A third way to persist objects is in the querystring. This makes for a long querystring. If you adopt this approach, I suggest that you introduce an object that represents a session and only contains "links" to objects in session. The link could be an object id. Store this session object in the querystring. You might look at encrypting the querystring.

Another way to persist objects is to serialise them into a database. To do this you need a table with a text field (text not varchar) and an identification field. You can use the unique id assigned to the User object in a varchar field as an identifier. Simply pass your serialized object to your insert query.

Chapter 6
Building Sites with the Object Factory

I find the usual "Hello World" examples unhelpful and inadequate for my purposes. I want to show you how quickly a site can be set up with this frame work. Let's build a typical business site that allows membership. It is a business that sells online by shipping product to online customers.

In order to ship product, the customer must supply a shipping address. The customer must pay before the shipment is sent.

Our site will be hosted on a Linux box by an Apache web server. Our development environment is a Windows2003 Server box with an Apache web server. We will develop in an Eclipse editor on a Window7 box. We're running PHP 5.2.13 and mySQL database on the Windows2003 Server box.

For this example I want to concentrate on getting the site functioning. Let us worry about the "Look" of the site after we know that everything works.

Most online business sites have a "Welcome" page as a landing (or home) page. I see this as a waste of time and space. The customer is visiting for one thing. Cheap goods. Forget the paradigm of fuzzy warm feelings being communicated verbally. A website will use color theory more effectively.

We want to give our customers what they want, so they will land on our "specials of the week" page. We will have a "Products" page, a "Contact" page, a "Help" page where we will offer advice on postage and handling. An "About" page will let the chairman have his say on company issues.

We will offer membership for a discount and use email addresses for our direct marketing campaign. We will have a payment gateway and SSL link.

All artwork to be supplied at a later date.

I want to make this example as realistic as possible. I will start at the point that I have extracted the ObjectFactory Frame Work from the downloaded file into a folder I created in my development environment called "BusinessExample.com"

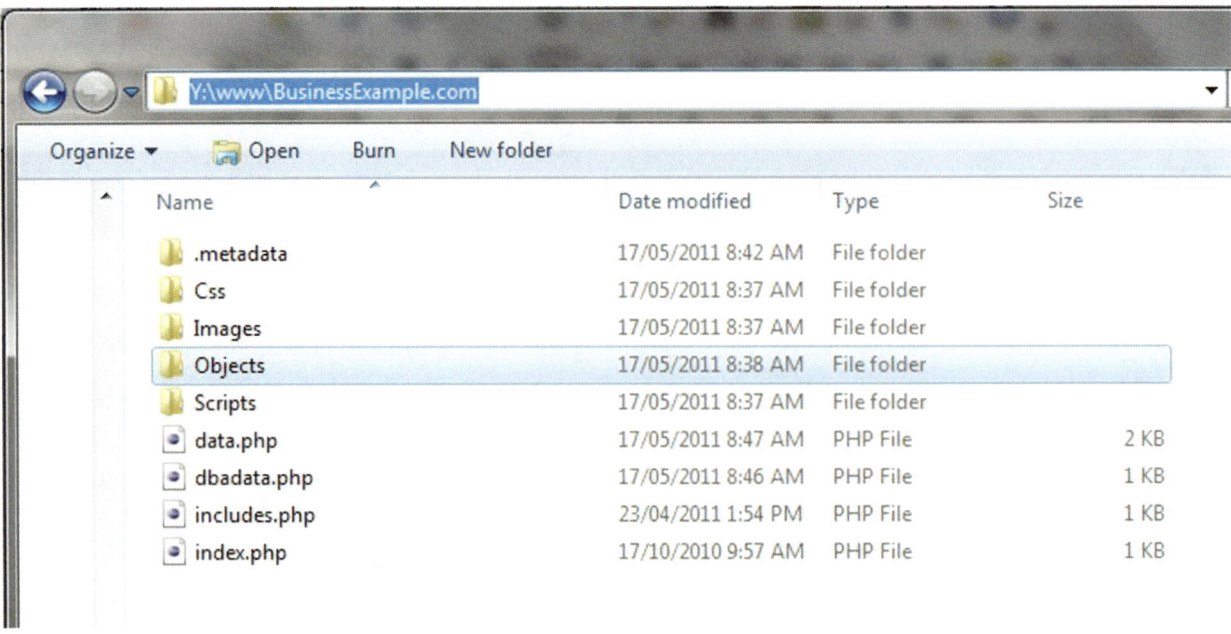

I open Eclipse and set my workbench accordingly.

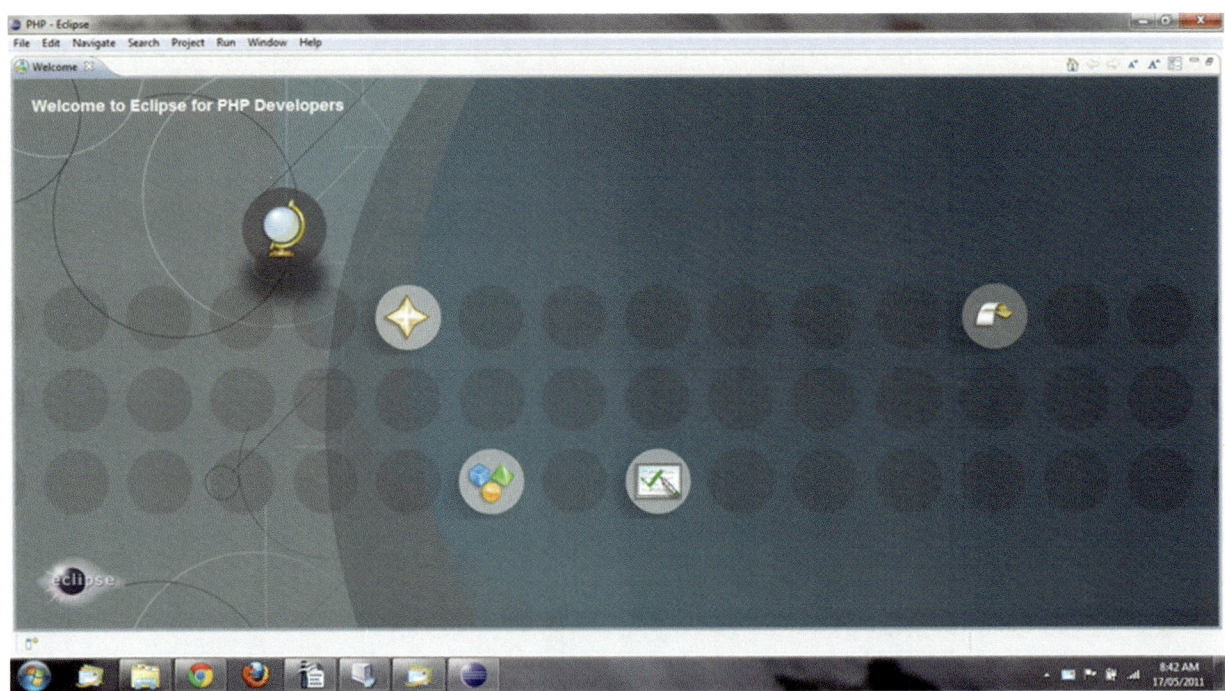

I open the four files I see in the root directory.

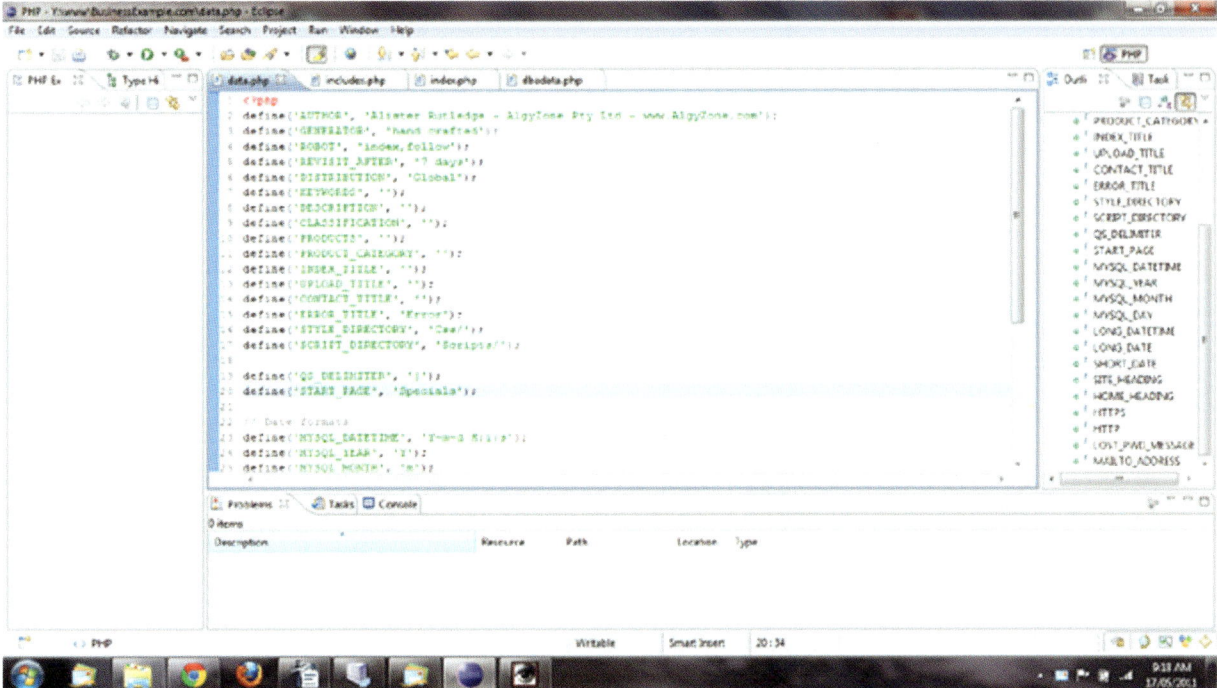

I find the constant START_PAGE and set it to 'Specials'

I hit the website with a browser.

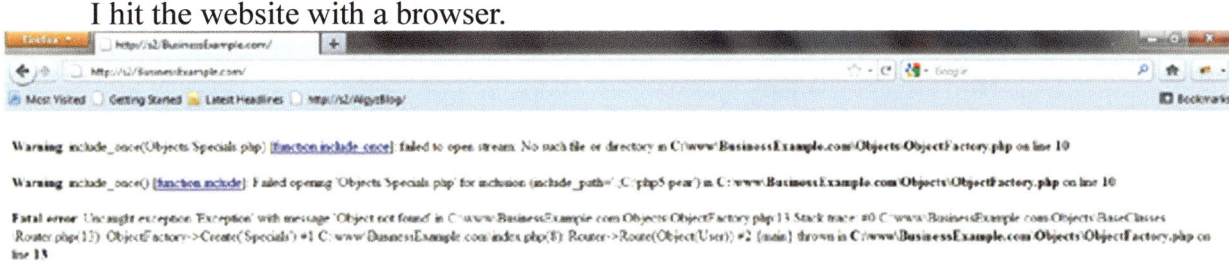

I throw a page not found error. The page I haven't found is "Specials.php" so I create a

new file in my Objects folder called "Specials.php".

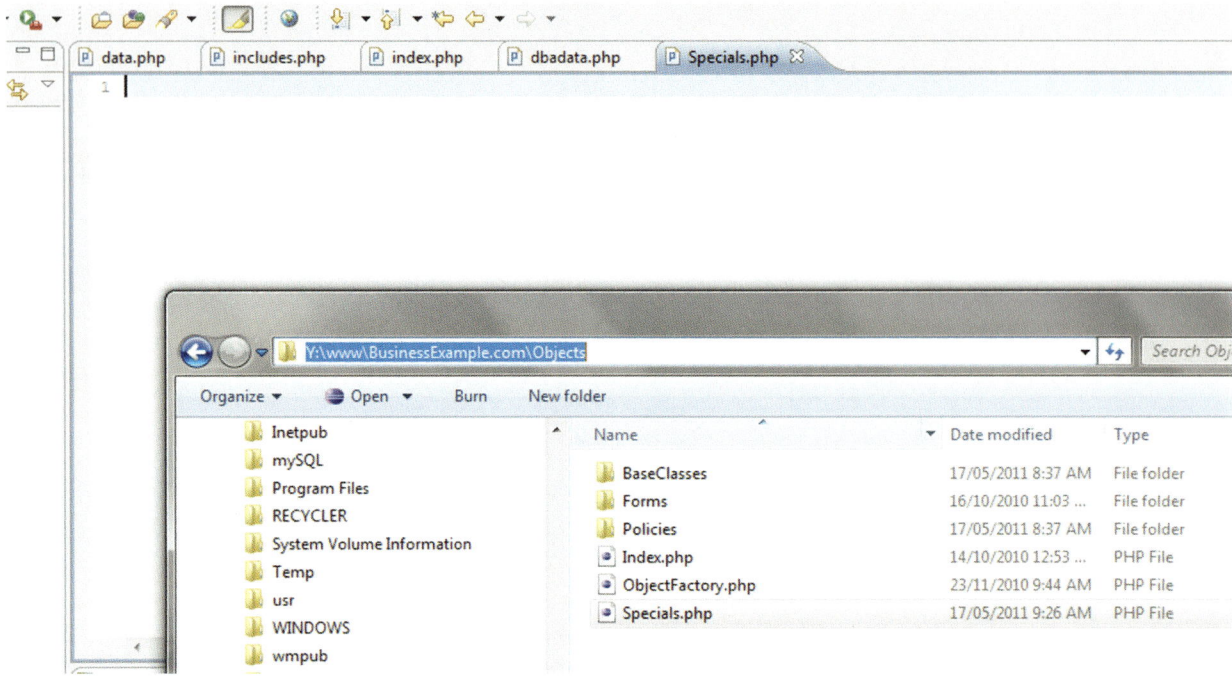

Now when I hit it with a web browser I get a different error message.

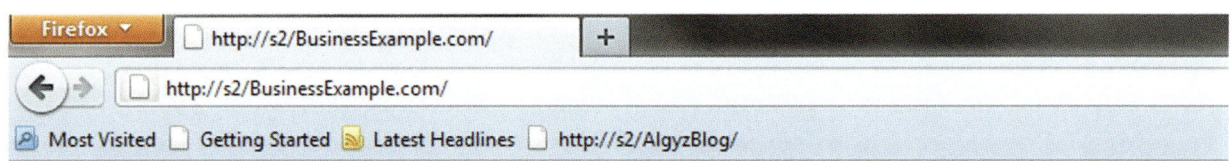

Fatal error: Class 'Specials' not found in **C:\www\BusinessExample.com\Objects\ObjectFactory.php** on line 11

Ok. So we found the file but not the object. That means the Framework is working. We want a Specials Object. We also want Products, Contact, Help and About objects. We also need to navigate between them.

I look in the BaseClasses folder and I open the Menu.php file.

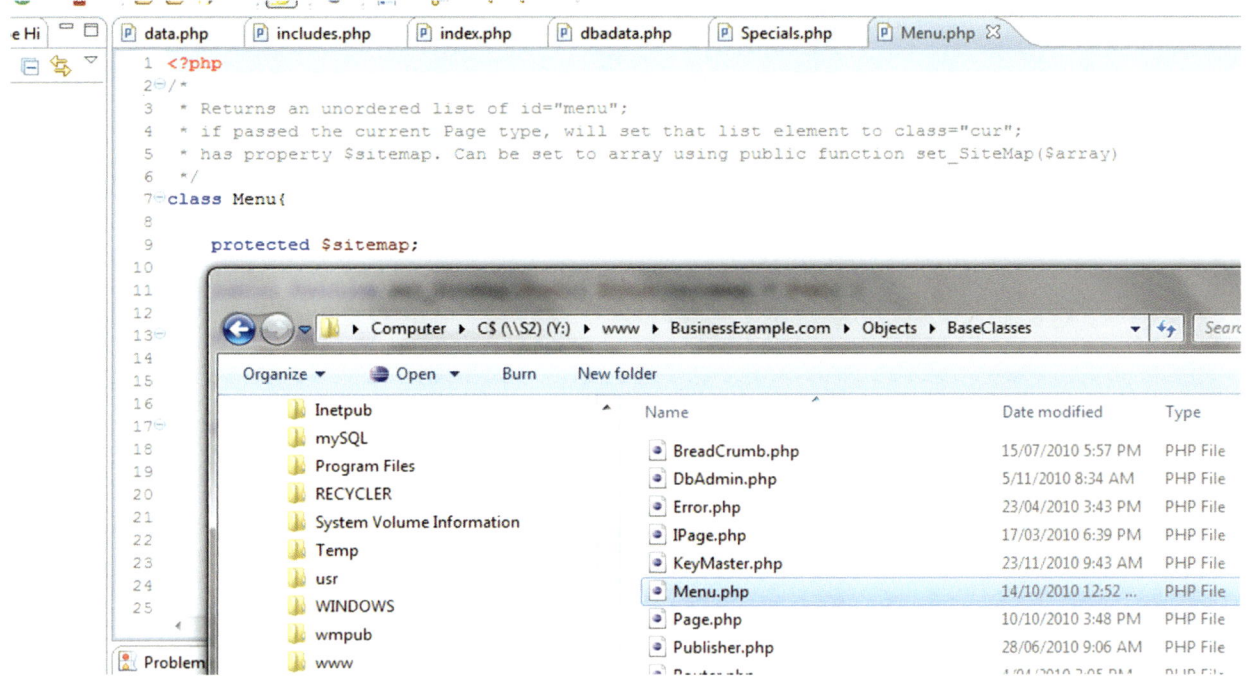

I change the sitemap parameter to contain the names of the objects I'm going to have on my site.

```php
4   * if passed the current Page type, will set that list element to class="cur";
5   * has property $sitemap. Can be set to array using public function set_SiteMap($array)
6   */
7   class Menu{

9       protected $sitemap;

11      public function set_SiteMap($val){ $this->sitemap = $val; }

13      public function __construct(){
14          $this->sitemap = array(START_PAGE, 'Products', 'Contact', 'Help', 'About');
15      }

17      public function writeNav($cur = 'null'){
```

I look in the Objects folder and I open the file called Index.php.

```php
1  <?php
2  class Index extends Page implements iPage{
3
4      protected $title;
5      protected $refresh;
6
7      public function get_Title(){
8          return $this->title;
9      }
10     public function get_Refresh(){
11         return $this->refresh;
12     }
13
14     public function __construct(){
15         $this->title = INDEX_TITLE;
16         $this->refresh = false;
17         parent::__construct();
18     }
19
20     public function Initialise(){
21         return parent::Initialise();
22     }
23
24     public function writeContent(){
25         return parent::writeMenu();
26     }
27
28     private function getMainContent(){
```

I see that the parent writeMenu() function is being invoked in the writeContent() method. I don't need to change any more code here for a menu to be displayed on this page. I will use this as a template to create my pages.

I copy and paste all the code from Index.php to Specials.php and change the class definition from `class Index`

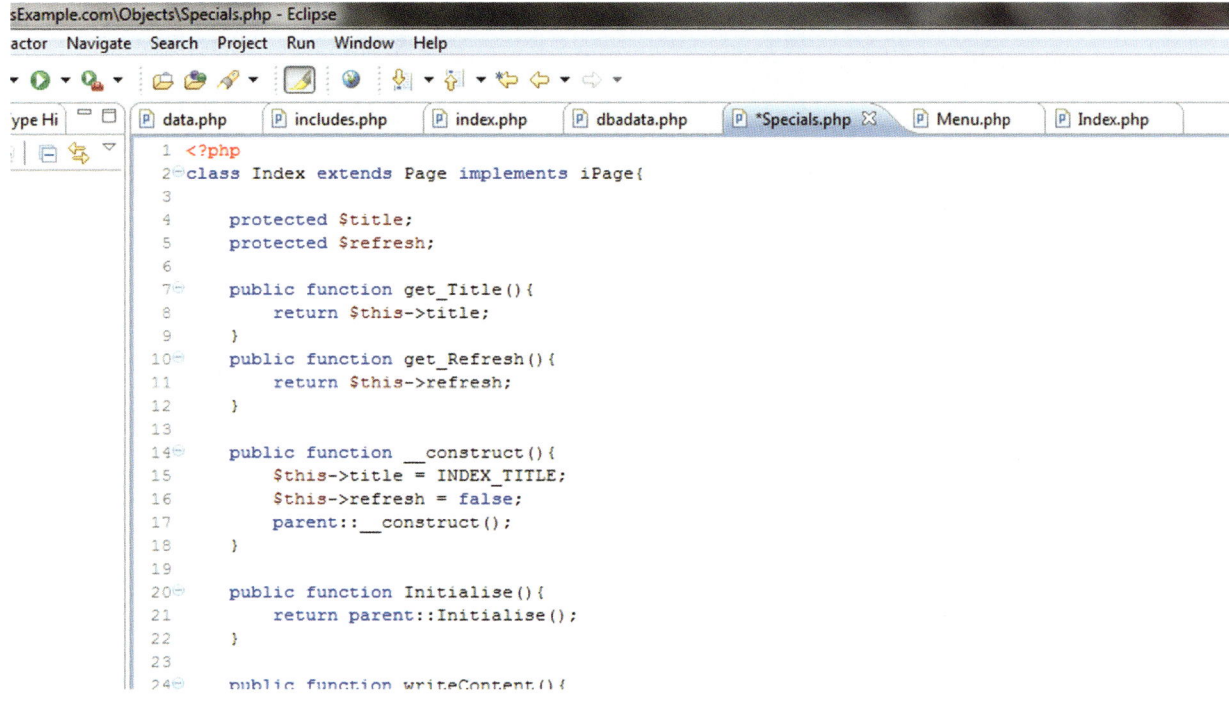

to `class Specials` and save it.

```php
<?php
class Specials extends Page implements iPage{

    protected $title;
    protected $refresh;

    public function get_Title(){
        return $this->title;
    }
    public function get_Refresh(){
        return $this->refresh;
    }

    public function __construct(){
        $this->title = INDEX_TITLE;
        $this->refresh = false;
        parent::__construct();
    }

    public function Initialise(){
        return parent::Initialise();
    }

    public function writeContent(){
```

Now I hit it with a web browser and I see a menu.

If I click on a link I get an error.

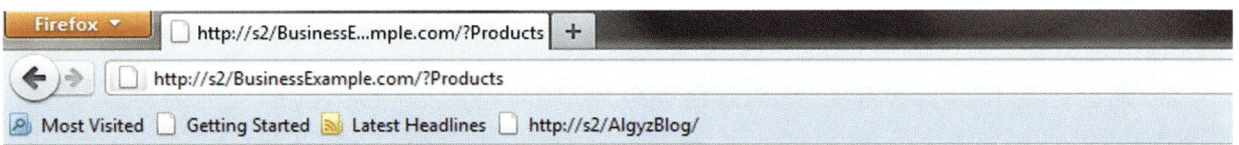

Warning: include_once(Objects/Products.php) [function.include-once]: failed to open stream: No such file or directory in C:\ww

Warning: include_once() [function.include]: Failed opening 'Objects/Products.php' for inclusion (include_path='.;C:\php5\pear') i

Fatal error: Uncaught exception 'Exception' with message 'Object not found' in C:\www\BusinessExample.com\Objects\ObjectI \Router.php(13): ObjectFactory->Create('Products') #1 C:\www\BusinessExample.com\index.php(8): Router->Route(Object(U

We've seen this before and know that if we create PHP files with the names in the menu, we will stop the error from occuring. I will create a Products.php file in the same way I created the Specials.php file.

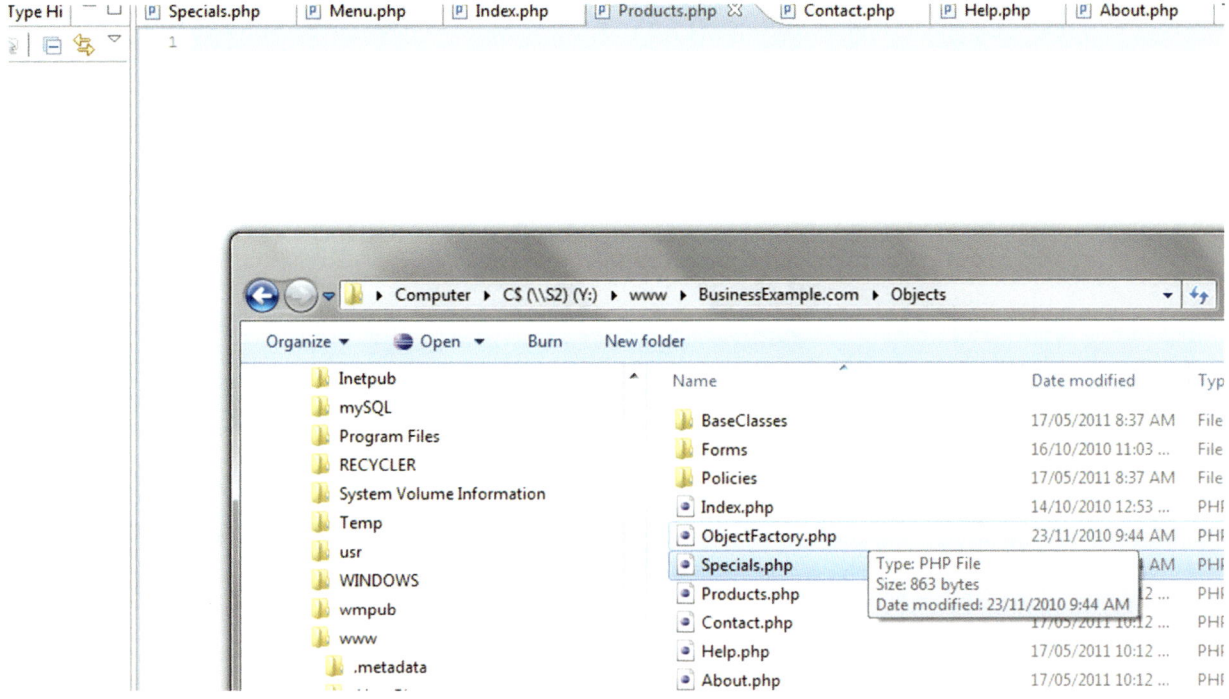

Now I'm going to copy and paste Index.php into my new files and change the class definition accordingly.

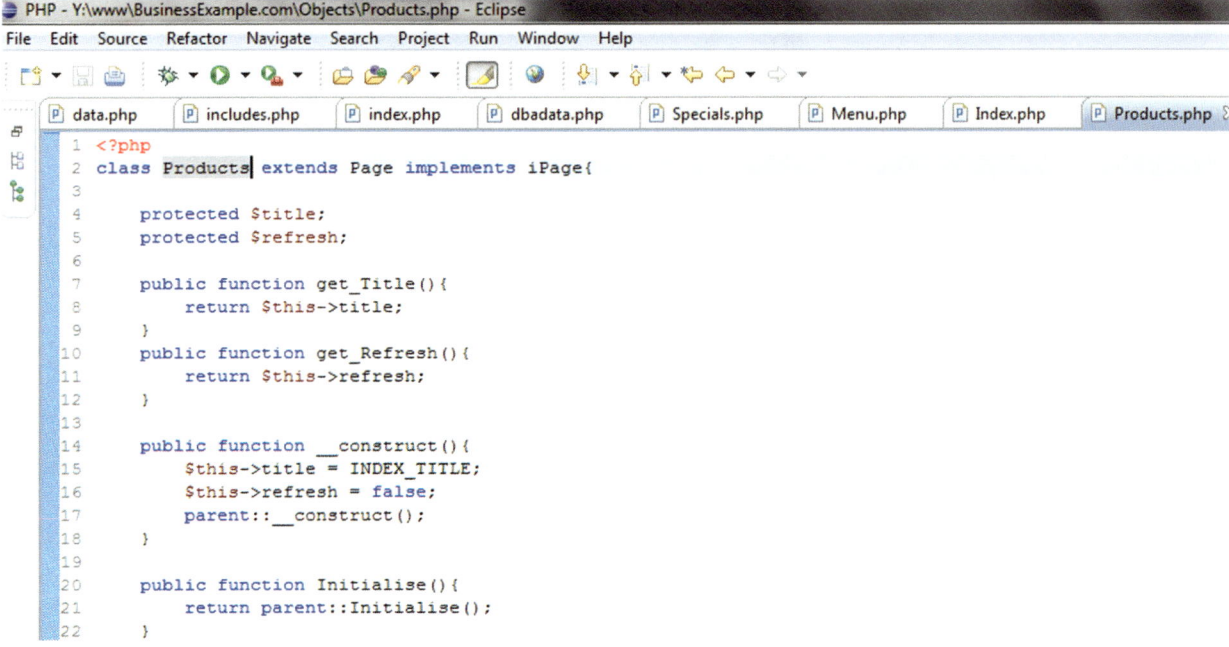

Now when I navigate about I don't see anything, but I don't throw any errors either.

Here's a blank Contact page. We've already seen the ContactForm object in action so what are we waiting for.

```php
14     public function __construct(){
15         $this->title = INDEX_TITLE;
16         $this->refresh = false;
17         parent::__construct();
18     }
19
20     public function Initialise(){
21         return parent::Initialise();
22     }
23
24     public function writeContent(){
25         return parent::writeMenu() . $this->getMainContent();
26     }
27
28     private function getMainContent(){
29         $obj = new ObjectFactory();
30         $frm = $obj->Create('ContactForm');
31         return $frm->writeForm();
32     }
33
34     public function Finalise(){
35         return  parent::Finalise();
36     }
```

I include the return value from the private method getMainContent() in the return value of writeContent(). In the getMainContent() function I include the three lines of code that create a contact form. When I hit it with a web browser.

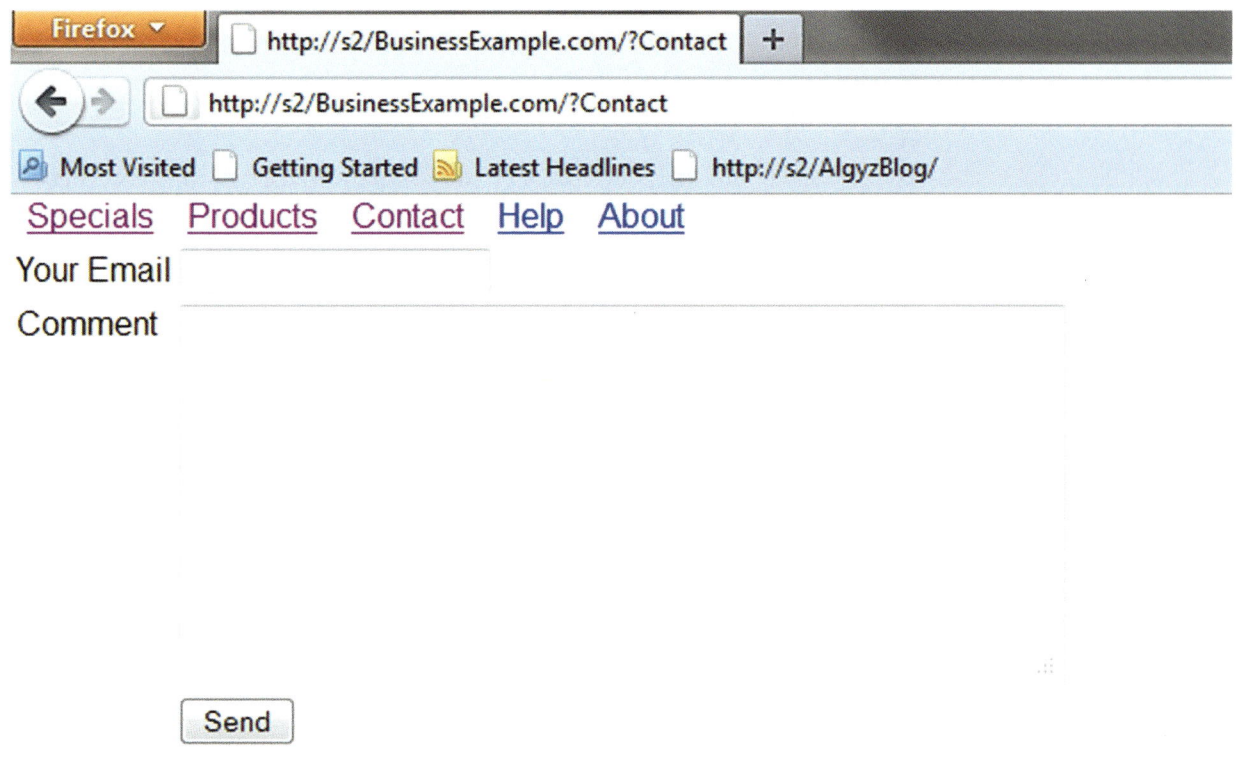

I see a contact form. I know that this form will actually send a valid email given valid input. I don't have to test this as I have seen the exact same code work on 5 previous sites. My Contact page is essentially complete with no further work required. Obviously some further work will be done on this page but it will be cosmetic only. This is a functioning contact page as is.

Our Specials and Products pages are going to display lists of products we have for sale in our business. All Product objects have several properties in common. A Product class can form a base class from which all Types can be derived. We create a page called Product.php in our editor.

```php
<?php
class Product{

    private $price;
    private $title;
    private $description;
    private $image;
    private $comment;

    public function get_Price(){ return $this->price; }
```

```php
        public function set_Price($pc){ $this->price = $pc; }
        public function get_Title(){ return $this->title; }
        public function set_Title($tt){ $this->title = $tt; }
        public function get_Description(){ return $this->description; }
        public function set_Description($dc){ $this->description = $dc; }
        public function get_Image(){ return $this->image; }
        public function set_Image($im){ $this->image = $im; }
        public function get_Comment(){ return $this->comment; }
        public function set_Comment($cmt){ $this->comment = $cmt; }

        public function __construct(){}

}
?>
```

Each product will have a price, title, description and image. Comment is there in case it's required.

The business will sell rubber ducks and feather dusters. A rubber duck looks like this;

```php
<?php
class RubberDuck extends Product{

        private $color;
        private $size;

        public function get_Color(){ return $this->color; }
        public function set_Color($cl){ $this->color = $cl; }
        public function get_Size(){ return $this->size; }
        public function set_Size($sz){$this->size = $sz; }

        public function __construct(){

        }

        public function Display(){
                $s = '<table class="product">
                        <tr><td>' . parent::get_Title() . '</td><td>' . parent::get_Price() .
'</td></tr>
                        <tr><td colspan="2">' . parent::get_Description() . '</td></tr>
                        <tr><td>Color: ' . $this->get_Color(). '</td><td>Size: ' . $this-
>get_Size() . '</td></tr>
                        <tr><td colspan="2">' . parent::get_Comment() . '</td></tr>
                        </table>';
                return $s;
        }

}
?>
```

A feather duster looks like this;

```php
<?php
class FeatherDuster extends Product{

        private $synthetic;

        public function get_Synthetic(){ return $this->synthetic; }
```

```php
public function set_Synthetic($sy){ $this->synthetic = $sy; }

public function __construct(){
        $this->synthetic = false;
        parent::__construct();
}

public function Display(){
        $s = '<table class="product"><tr>
                    <td>' . parent::get_Title() . '</td><td>' . parent::get_Price() .
'</td></tr>
                    <tr><td colspan="2">' . parent::get_Description() . '</td></tr>
                    <tr><td>' . $this->get_Synthetic() . '</td><td></td></tr>
                    <tr><td colspan="2">' . parent::get_Comment() . '</td>
            </tr></table>';
        return $s;
}

}
?>
```

Each sub class of Product knows how to display itself on the page and has extra properties.

We go back to our Specials page and make some changes.

```php
 5              return parent::writeMenu() . $this->getMainContent();
 6        }
 7
 8⊖     private function getMainContent(){
 9            $s = '<div id="specials">';
 0            $obj = new ObjectFactory();
 1            $dba = $obj->Create('DbAdmin');
 2            $rs = $dba->getSoftware('specials');
 3            if($rs){
 4                for($i=0;$i<mysql_num_rows($rs);$i++){
 5                    $row = mysql_fetch_row($rs);
 6                    if($row[0] == 'Rubber Duck'){
 7                        $sp = $obj->Create('RubberDuck');
 8                    }else{
 9                        $sp = $obj->Create('FeatherDuster');
 0                    }
 1                    $sp->set_Title($row[0]);
 2                    $sp->set_Price($row[1]);
 3                    $sp->set_Description($row[2]);
 4                    if($row[0] == 'Rubber Duck'){
 5                        $sp->set_Color($row[4]);
 6                        $sp->set_Size($row[5]);
 7                    }else{
 8                        $sp->set_Synthetic($row[4]);
 9                    }
 0                    $sp->set_Comment($row[3]);
 1                    $s .= $sp->Display() . '<br /><br />';
 2                }
 3            }
 4            return $s . '</div>';
 5        }
```

In the getMainContent() function we open a <div> element and create an ObjectFactory. We ask the $obj ObjectFactory to create a DbAdmin object. We ask the $dba DbAdmin object to getSoftware('specials') and assign the value returned to $rs.

The DbAdmin object extends the State object and resides in the BaseClasses subfolder. It extends the State object because it uses the State's database connection.

We open the DbAdmin.php file in our editor and add a function;

```php
public function getProducts($type){
    $query = "SELECT * FROM products WHERE type = '" . $type . "'";
```

```
        return $this->getRecords($query);
}
```

DbAdmin has three private functions.

```
private function getRecords($query){
        $conn = parent::DbConn();
        if($conn){
                $rs = mysql_query($query, $conn);
                if(mysql_errno() > 0){
                        $this->DbError(mysql_error());
                }else{
                        return $rs;
                }
        }
        return null;
}


private function runSelect($query){
        $conn = parent::DbConn();
        if($conn){
                $rs = mysql_query($query, $conn);
                if(mysql_errno() > 0){
                        $this->DbError(mysql_error());
                }
                return true;
        }
        return false;
}


private function DbError($msg){
        $obj = new ObjectFactory();
        $sm = $obj->Create('SiteManager');
        $pge = $obj->Create('Error');
        $user = $obj->Create('User');
        $pge->set_Message($msg);
        $user->set_PageType('Error');
        $pge->set_User($user);
        $sm->Manage($pge);
        die();
}
```

To use it, you create a public function that builds the required query string and invoke either runSelect() or getRecords() as required.

DbError() is an example of object level redirection that the framework can do. A SiteManager object is created and a Page of Type Error is created. A User is created. It's PageType is set to Error. The Error Page has a message property that is set to $msg. The User is assigned to the Error Page's user property and then the SiteManager is asked to Manage it in the usual manner. After which the die() directive is issued, stopping further processing of the current script.

Now when we go back to our Specials page;

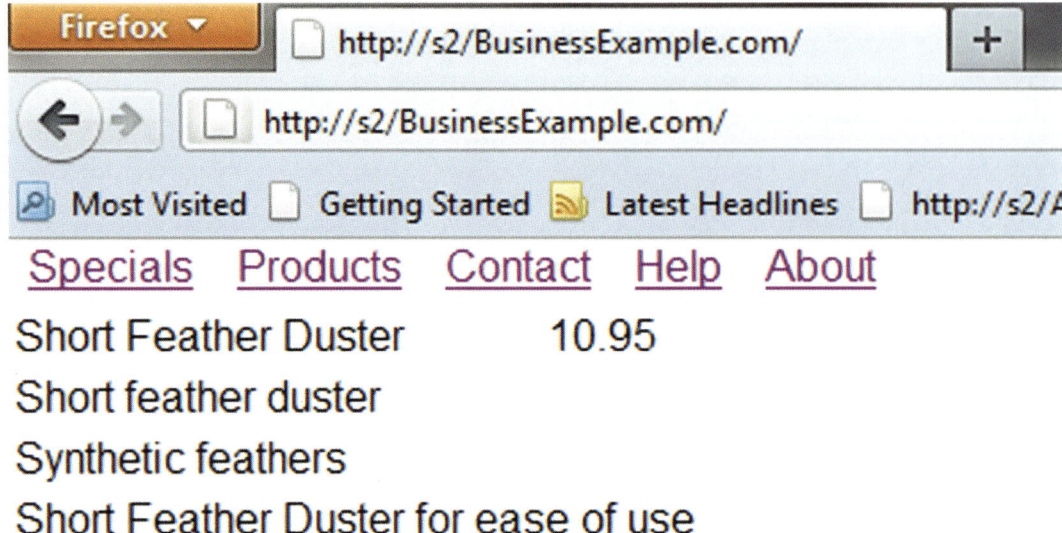

We have a couple of specials. Images to be supplied by the Marketing department. Products is next. We are going to tackle it in the same way we developed Specials.

I go to my Products.php file and make the following changes;

```php
private function getMainContent(){
    $s = '<div id="products">';
    $obj = new ObjectFactory();
    $dba = $obj->Create('DbAdmin');
    $rs = $dba->getProducts('Rubber Duck');
    if($rs){
```

```php
        for($i=0;$i<mysql_num_rows($rs);$i++){
                $row = mysql_fetch_row($rs);
                $p = $obj->Create('RubberDuck');
                $p->set_Title($row[1]);
                $p->set_Price($row[2]);
                $p->set_Description($row[3]);
                $p->set_Color($row[4]);
                $p->set_Size($row[5]);
                $p->set_Comment($row[7]);
                $s .= $p->Display() . '<br /><br />';
        }
    }
    $rs = $dba->getProducts('Feather Duster');
    if($rs){
        for($i=0;$i<mysql_num_rows($rs);$i++){
                $row = mysql_fetch_row($rs);
                $p = $obj->Create('FeatherDuster');
                $p->set_Title($row[1]);
                $p->set_Price($row[2]);
                $p->set_Description($row[3]);
                $p->set_Synthetic($row[6]);
                $p->set_Comment($row[7]);
                $s .= $p->Display() . '<br /><br />';
        }
    }
    return $s . '</div>';
}
```

We go back to our browser and hit the Products page;

Specials   Products   Contact   Help   About

Red Rubber Duck   12.95
Big friendly red rubber duck
Color: Red   Size: Large
Big red rubber duck for all your red rubber duck needs

Blue Rubber Duck   12.95
Medium friendly blue rubber duck
Color: Blue   Size: Medium
Medium blue rubber duck for all your blue rubber duck needs

Long Feather Duster   12.95
Long feather duster
Real feathers
Long Feather Duster for better reach

Short Feather Duster   12.95
Short feather duster
Synthetic feathers
Short Feather Duster for ease of use

We have a list of Rubber Ducks and Feather Dusters. What about images of our products? The Marketing department has not yet supplied the required image files but there is no need for the developers to be held back by this.

Our Product objects don't have the ability to display images yet, so let's implement that now. We go back to our Feather Duster object and add an image tag;

```php
public function Display(){
        $s = '<div><img src="' . parent::get_Image() . '" alt="Feather Duster Image" />
                <table class="product">
                <tr><td>' . parent::get_Title() . '</td><td>' .
parent::get_Price() . '</td></tr>
                <tr><td colspan="2">' . parent::get_Description() . '</td></tr>
                <tr><td>' . $this->get_Synthetic() . '</td><td></td></tr>
                <tr><td colspan="2">' . parent::get_Comment() . '</td>
        </tr></table></div>';
        return $s;
    }
```

We do the same for our Rubber Ducks;

```php
public function Display(){
        $s = '<div><img src="' . parent::get_Image() . '" alt="Rubber Duck Image" />
                <table class="product">
                <tr><td>' . parent::get_Title() . '</td><td>' .
parent::get_Price() . '</td></tr>
                <tr><td colspan="2">' . parent::get_Description() . '</td></tr>
                <tr><td>Color: ' . $this->get_Color(). '</td><td>Size: ' . $this->get_Size() . '</td></tr>
                <tr><td colspan="2">' . parent::get_Comment() . '</td></tr>
            </table></div>';
        return $s;
    }
```

When we visit our browser again we see the alt attribute value which will be replaced with an image once they are supplied by the marketing department.

Specials   Products   Contact   Help   About

Rubber Duck Image
Red Rubber Duck   12.95
Big friendly red rubber duck
Color: Red   Size: Large
Big red rubber duck for all your red rubber duck needs

Rubber Duck Image
Blue Rubber Duck   12.95
Medium friendly blue rubber duck
Color: Blue   Size: Medium
Medium blue rubber duck for all your blue rubber duck needs

Feather Duster Image
Long Feather Duster   12.95
Long feather duster
Real feathers
Long Feather Duster for better reach

Feather Duster Image
Short Feather Duster   12.95
Short feather duster
Synthetic feathers
Short Feather Duster for ease of use

In about 30 minutes we have created the front end of a commercial website. If we want to add more Rubber Ducks or Feather Dusters to our inventory, we only need to enter the relevant parameters to our database. No changes to the code are required. That means we can scale up our inventory without testing any code.

So far, so good, but we still can't take any money through our site. We need a shopping cart and a checkout. We also need to take billing address details and credit card payments.

We need to adjust our Rubber Ducks and Feather Dusters. We add a link to the shopping cart under the product price. But first we'll need to uniquely identify each product. Each product requires a unique id so we adjust the Product base class.

```php
<?php
class Product{

    private $id;
    private $price;
    private $title;
    private $description;
    private $image;
    private $comment;

    public function set_Id($ident){ $this->id = $ident; }
    public function get_Id(){ return $this->id; }
    public function get_Price(){ return $this->price; }
    public function set_Price($pc){ $this->price = $pc; }
    public function get_Title(){ return $this->title; }
    public function set_Title($tt){ $this->title = $tt; }
    public function get_Description(){ return $this->description; }
    public function set_Description($dc){ $this->description = $dc; }
    public function get_Image(){ return $this->image; }
    public function set_Image($im){ $this->image = $im; }
    public function get_Comment(){ return $this->comment; }
    public function set_Comment($cmt){ $this->comment = $cmt; }

    public function __construct(){}

}
?>
```

We add an $id property to our Product class.

We add a link to the FeatherDuster and RubberDuck objects.

```php
<?php
class FeatherDuster extends Product{

    private $synthetic;

    public function get_Synthetic(){ return $this->synthetic; }
    public function set_Synthetic($sy){ $this->synthetic = $sy; }
```

```php
        public function __construct(){
                $this->synthetic = false;
                parent::__construct();
        }

        public function Display(){
                $s = '<div><img src="' . parent::get_Image() . '" alt="Feather Duster Image" />
                            <table class="product">
                            <tr><td>' . parent::get_Title() . '</td><td>' .
parent::get_Price() . '<br />
                                <a href="?' . parent::get_Id() . '/addtocart/Products">Add to
Shopping Cart</a></td></tr>
                            <tr><td colspan="2">' . parent::get_Description() . '</td></tr>
                            <tr><td>' . $this->get_Synthetic() . '</td><td></td></tr>
                            <tr><td colspan="2">' . parent::get_Comment() . '</td>
                </tr></table></div>';
                return $s;
        }

}
?>


<?php
class RubberDuck extends Product{

        private $color;
        private $size;

        public function get_Color(){ return $this->color; }
        public function set_Color($cl){ $this->color = $cl; }
        public function get_Size(){ return $this->size; }
        public function set_Size($sz){$this->size = $sz; }

        public function __construct(){

        }

        public function Display(){
                $s = '<div><img src="' . parent::get_Image() . '" alt="Rubber Duck Image" />
                            <table class="product">
                            <tr><td>' . parent::get_Title() . '</td><td>' .
parent::get_Price() . '<br />
                                <a href="?' . parent::get_Id() . '/addtocart/Products">Add to
Shopping Cart</a></td></tr>
                            <tr><td colspan="2">' . parent::get_Description() . '</td></tr>
                            <tr><td>Color: ' . $this->get_Color(). '</td><td>Size: ' . $this-
>get_Size() . '</td></tr>
                            <tr><td colspan="2">' . parent::get_Comment() . '</td></tr>
                        </table></div>';
                return $s;
        }

}
?>
```

We go back to our Specials and Products Page objects and assign the database id field to our new $id properties.

```php
        private function getMainContent(){
                $s = '<div id="specials">';
                $obj = new ObjectFactory();
                $dba = $obj->Create('DbAdmin');
```

```php
        $rs = $dba->getProducts('Special');
        if($rs){
                for($i=0;$i<mysql_num_rows($rs);$i++){
                        $row = mysql_fetch_row($rs);
                        if($row[9] == 'Rubber Duck'){
                                $sp = $obj->Create('RubberDuck');
                        }else{
                                $sp = $obj->Create('FeatherDuster');
                        }
                        $sp->set_Id($row[0]);
                        $sp->set_Title($row[1]);
                        $sp->set_Price($row[2]);
                        $sp->set_Description($row[3]);
                        if($row[0] == 'Rubber Duck'){
                                $sp->set_Color($row[4]);
                                $sp->set_Size($row[5]);
                        }else{
                                $sp->set_Synthetic($row[6]);
                        }
                        $sp->set_Comment($row[7]);
                        $s .= $sp->Display() . '<br /><br />';
                }
        }
        return $s . '</div>';
}


        if($rs){
                for($i=0;$i<mysql_num_rows($rs);$i++){
                        $row = mysql_fetch_row($rs);
                        $p = $obj->Create('RubberDuck');
                        $p->set_Id($row[0]);
                        $p->set_Title($row[1]);
                        $p->set_Price($row[2]);
                        $p->set_Description($row[3]);
                        $p->set_Color($row[4]);
                        $p->set_Size($row[5]);
                        $p->set_Comment($row[7]);
                        $s .= $p->Display() . '<br /><br />';
                }
        }
        $rs = $dba->getProducts('Feather Duster');
        if($rs){
                for($i=0;$i<mysql_num_rows($rs);$i++){
                        $row = mysql_fetch_row($rs);
                        $p = $obj->Create('FeatherDuster');
                        $p->set_Id($row[0]);
                        $p->set_Title($row[1]);
                        $p->set_Price($row[2]);
                        $p->set_Description($row[3]);
                        $p->set_Synthetic($row[6]);
                        $p->set_Comment($row[7]);
```

```
                    $s .= $p->Display() . '<br /><br />';
        }
```

When we hit Specials with the web browser we see;

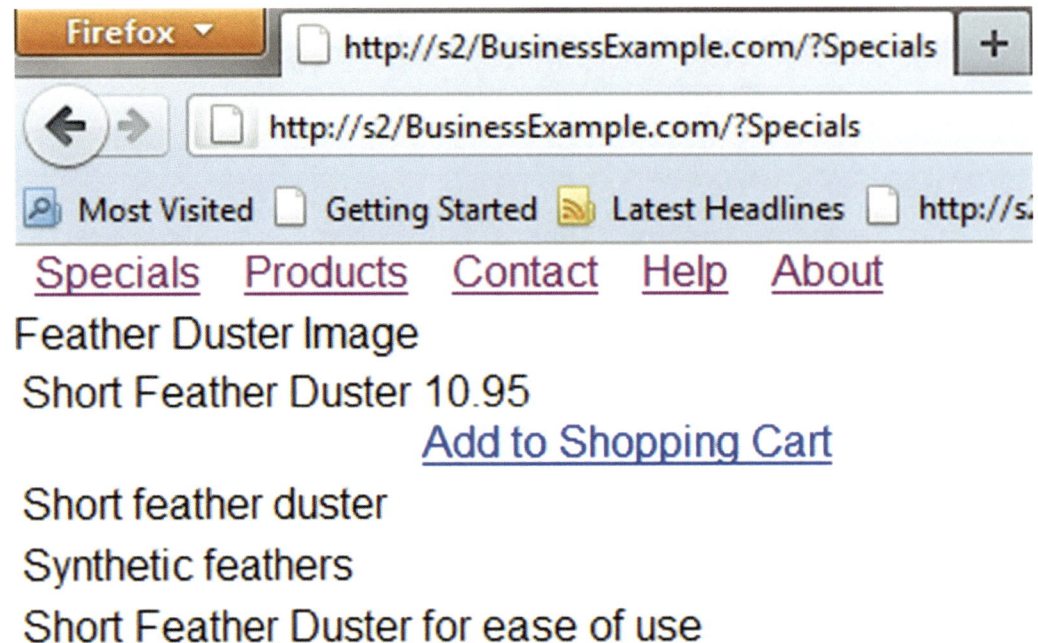

And Products;

Specials   Products   Contact   Help   About

Rubber Duck Image
Red Rubber Duck   12.95
                         Add to Shopping Cart
Big friendly red rubber duck
Color: Red   Size: Large
Big red rubber duck for all your red rubber duck needs

Rubber Duck Image
Blue Rubber Duck   12.95
                          Add to Shopping Cart
Medium friendly blue rubber duck
Color: Blue   Size: Medium
Medium blue rubber duck for all your blue rubber duck needs

Feather Duster Image
Long Feather Duster 12.95
                          Add to Shopping Cart
Long feather duster
Real feathers
Long Feather Duster for better reach

Feather Duster Image
Short Feather Duster 12.95
                          Add to Shopping Cart
Short feather duster
Synthetic feathers

We will need to add a shopping cart table to our database;

```sql
CREATE TABLE `shoppingcart` (
`id` bigint(20) unsigned NOT NULL auto_increment,
`userid` varchar(40) NOT NULL,
`productid` bigint NOT NULL,
`timeentered` datetime NOT NULL,
`paid` tinyint(4) NOT NULL default '0',
PRIMARY KEY  (`id`)
) ENGINE=MyISAM  DEFAULT CHARSET=latin1
```

Now we go back to our Specials page and make some changes;

```php
<?php
class Specials extends Page implements iPage{

        protected $title;
        protected $refresh;
        private $qs;
        private $cart;

        public function get_Title(){
                return $this->title;
        }
        public function get_Refresh(){
                return $this->refresh;
        }
        public function get_Cart(){
                return $this->cart;
        }

        public function __construct(){
                $this->title = INDEX_TITLE;
                $this->refresh = false;
                $obj = new ObjectFactory();
                $this->cart = $obj->Create('ShoppingCart');
                parent::__construct();
        }

        public function Initialise(){
                $this->cart->CheckItems(parent::get_User()->get_UserId());
                $this->qs = explode(QS_DELIMITER, $_SERVER['QUERY_STRING']);
                if(count($this->qs) > 1){
                        $obj = new ObjectFactory();
                        $dba = $obj->Create('DbAdmin');
                        if($this->qs[1] == 'addtocart'){
                                $dba->AddToCart(addslashes($this->qs[0]), parent::get_User()-
>get_UserId());
                                $this->cart->Add_Item(addslashes($this->qs[0]));
                        }
                }
                return parent::Initialise();
        }

        public function writeContent(){
                return parent::writeMenu() . $this->getMainContent();
        }
```

```php
        private function getMainContent(){
                $s = '<div id="shoppingcart">';
                if($this->cart->ItemCount() > 0){
                        $s .= $this->cart->DisplayCart();
                }
                $s .= '</div>';
                $s .= '<div id="specials">';
                $obj = new ObjectFactory();
                $dba = $obj->Create('DbAdmin');
                $rs = $dba->getProducts('Special');
                if($rs){
                        for($i=0;$i<mysql_num_rows($rs);$i++){
                                $row = mysql_fetch_row($rs);
                                if($row[9] == 'Rubber Duck'){
                                        $sp = $obj->Create('RubberDuck');
                                }else{
                                        $sp = $obj->Create('FeatherDuster');
                                }
                                $sp->set_Id($row[0]);
                                $sp->set_Title($row[1]);
                                $sp->set_Price($row[2]);
                                $sp->set_Description($row[3]);
                                if($row[0] == 'Rubber Duck'){
                                        $sp->set_Color($row[4]);
                                        $sp->set_Size($row[5]);
                                }else{
                                        $sp->set_Synthetic($row[6]);
                                }
                                $sp->set_Comment($row[7]);
                                $s .= $sp->Display() . '<br /><br />';
                        }
                }
                return $s . '</div>';
        }

        public function Finalise(){
                return  parent::Finalise();
        }

        protected function onBeforeContent(){
                return '<div>Blah Blah Blah Blah Blah Blah Blah Blah Blah Blah Blah Blah Blah
</div>';
        }

        protected function onAfterContent(){
                return '<div>Blah Blah Blah Blah Blah Blah Blah Blah Blah Blah Blah Blah Blah
</div>';
        }

}
?>
```

We have added two new properties;

```php
private $qs;
private $cart;
```

and one accessor;

```php
public function get_Cart(){
        return $this->cart;
```

```
            }
```

In our constructor, we have created a ShoppingCart object and assigned it to $cart;

```php
$obj = new ObjectFactory();
$this->cart = $obj->Create('ShoppingCart');
```

When the Specials Page initialises we will now check our shopping cart and check if we are adding items to our shopping cart;

```php
$this->cart->CheckItems(parent::get_User()->get_UserId());
$this->qs = explode(QS_DELIMITER, $_SERVER['QUERY_STRING']);
if(count($this->qs) > 1){
        $obj = new ObjectFactory();
        $dba = $obj->Create('DbAdmin');
        if($this->qs[1] == 'addtocart'){
                $dba->AddToCart(addslashes($this->qs[0]),
parent::get_User()->get_UserId());
                $this->cart->Add_Item(addslashes($this->qs[0]));
        }
}
```

We can see that our DbAdmin will need to have an AddToCart() method created. Our ShoppingCart object is found in the BaseClasses folder and looks like this;

```php
<?php
class ShoppingCart{

    private $items;
    private $userid;

    public function Add_Item($id){
            $this->items[] = $id;
    }

    public function Remove_Item($id){
            unset($this->items[$id]);
    }

    public function __construct(){

    }

    public function ItemCount(){
            return count($this->items);
    }

    public function DisplayCart($heading = false){
            $s = '<table summary="layout" class="cart">';
            if($heading){
                    $s .= '<tr><td>Shopping Cart</td></tr>';
            }
            $s .= '<tr><td>';
            $s .= $this->ItemCount();
            $s .= ($this->ItemCount() == 1)? ' Item':' Items';
            $s .= '</td></tr>
                    <tr><td><a href="?DisplayItems/CheckOut" class="display">Proceed to
```

```php
Checkout</a></td></tr></table>';
            return $s;
    }

    public function CheckItems($uid){
            $this->userid = $uid;
            $query = "SELECT productid FROM shoppingcart WHERE TRIM(userid) = '" . $uid . "'
AND paid = 0";
            $rs = $this->getRecords($query);
            if(mysql_num_rows($rs) > 0){
                    for($i=0;$i<mysql_num_rows($rs);$i++){
                            $row = mysql_fetch_row($rs);
                            $this->items[] = $row[0];
                    }
            }
    }

    private function getRecords($query){
            $conn = $this->DbConn();
            if($conn){
                    $rs = mysql_query($query, $conn);
                    if(mysql_errno() > 0){
                            $this->DbError(mysql_error());
                    }else{
                            return $rs;
                    }
            }
            return null;
    }

    private function runSelect($query){
            $conn = $this->DbConn();
            if($conn){
                    $rs = mysql_query($query, $conn);
                    if(mysql_errno() > 0){
                            $this->DbError(mysql_error());
                    }
                    return true;
            }
            return false;
    }

    private function DbError($msg){
            $obj = new ObjectFactory();
            $sm = $obj->Create('SiteManager');
            $pge = $obj->Create('Error');
            $user = $obj->Create('User');
            $pge->set_Message($msg);
            $user->set_PageType('Error');
            $pge->set_User($user);
            $sm->Manage($pge);
            die();
    }

    private function DbConn(){
            $conn = mysql_connect(SERVER, STATE_USER, STATE_PWD) or die ('I cannot connect to
the database because: ' . mysql_error());
            mysql_select_db (DATABASE);
            if($conn){
                    return $conn;
            }else{
                    return null;
            }
    }

}
?>
```

There is really nothing new in this object. It follows the standard structure of a smart object. It can perform all the tasks that a ShoppingCart requires including displaying it's self on the screen.

Our DbAdmin object requires a method to add items to the table created above and we might as well add a method to remove items at the same time. We add the following functions to the DbAdmin object;

```
public function AddToCart($aid, $uid){
        $query = "INSERT INTO shoppingcart (userid, productid, timeentered)
        VALUES ('" . $uid . "', '" . $aid . "', '" . date(MYSQL_DATETIME) . "')";
        $this->runSelect($query);
}

public function RemoveFromCart($id, $uid){
        $query = "DELETE FROM shoppingcart WHERE id = " . $id . " AND TRIM(userid) = '" .
$uid . "'";
        return $this->runSelect($query);
}
```

Now when we click on any Add to Shopping Cart link on the Specials page we see;

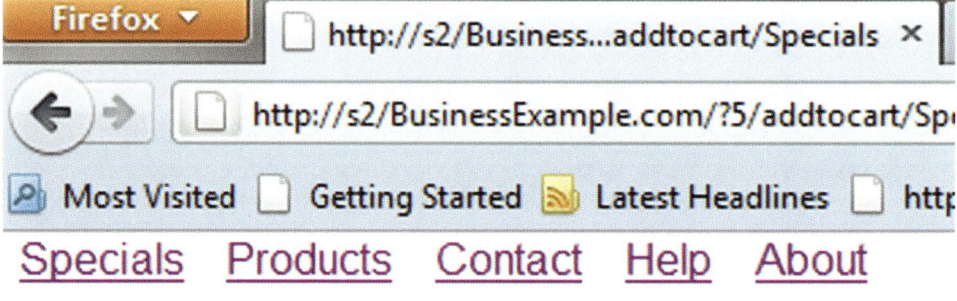

Specials   Products   Contact   Help   About

Shopping Cart

1 Item

Proceed to Checkout

Feather Duster Image

Short Feather Duster 10.95

Add to Shopping Cart

Short feather duster

Synthetic feathers

Short Feather Duster for ease of use

Admittedly the page looks terrible, but remember, form follows function. Right now we have spent 45 minutes developing an eCommerce site and we only have checkout and credit card payment to go.

If the project time line is 3 months, it can mostly be spent making the site look pretty and snow boarding. The site is operational to this point.

Let's update the Products page with the same code changes we made to Specials.

```php
private function getMainContent(){
        $s = '<div id="shoppingcart">Shopping Cart<br />';
        if($this->cart->ItemCount() > 0){
                $s .= $this->cart->DisplayCart();
            }
        $s .= '</div>';
        $s .= '<div id="products">';
        $obj = new ObjectFactory();
        $dba = $obj->Create('DbAdmin');
        $rs = $dba->getProducts('Rubber Duck');
        if($rs){
                for($i=0;$i<mysql_num_rows($rs);$i++){
                        $row = mysql_fetch_row($rs);
                        $p = $obj->Create('RubberDuck');
                        $p->set_Id($row[0]);
                        $p->set_Title($row[1]);
                        $p->set_Price($row[2]);
                        $p->set_Description($row[3]);
                        $p->set_Color($row[4]);
                        $p->set_Size($row[5]);
                        $p->set_Comment($row[7]);
                        $s .= $p->Display(parent::get_User()->get_PageType()) . '<br /><br
/>';
                }
        }
        $rs = $dba->getProducts('Feather Duster');
        if($rs){
                for($i=0;$i<mysql_num_rows($rs);$i++){
                        $row = mysql_fetch_row($rs);
                        $p = $obj->Create('FeatherDuster');
                        $p->set_Id($row[0]);
                        $p->set_Title($row[1]);
                        $p->set_Price($row[2]);
                        $p->set_Description($row[3]);
                        $p->set_Synthetic($row[6]);
                        $p->set_Comment($row[7]);
                        $s .= $p->Display(parent::get_User()->get_PageType()) . '<br /><br
/>';
                }
        }
        return $s . '</div>';
    }
```

When we add a product to the shopping cart we see

Specials   Products   Contact   Help   About

Shopping Cart

1 Item

Proceed to Checkout

Rubber Duck Image

Red Rubber Duck   12.95

Add to Shopping Cart

Big friendly red rubber duck

Color: Red   Size: Large

Big red rubber duck for all your red rubber duck needs

Rubber Duck Image

Blue Rubber Duck   12.95

Add to Shopping Cart

Medium friendly blue rubber duck

Color: Blue   Size: Medium

Medium blue rubber duck for all your blue rubber duck needs

Now we need a check out so that users can remove items from their shopping cart if they desire. Let's take a step back for a minute and consider what happens at a supermarket checkout. The customer wheels their shopping cart up to the checkout counter and puts the items on the conveyor belt. The checkout chick totals up the items and the customer pays for them.

OOD is about modeling the real world through objects. So what do we have. We have a

User object and a ShoppingCart object. A CheckOut object will need to be a Page Type object as we have to show the items on the conveyor to our customer.

The process is a linear one and our User should not be able to reach the Checkout without firstly putting something in the ShoppingCart. So we don't want our ShoppingCart accessable via the menu bar. We have that functionality already built into our ShoppingCart object by means of the Proceed to Check Out link.

However, once the customer is at the CheckOut, we want to give the User the ability to abandon the ShoppingCart without getting lost. Our CheckOut needs to display the menu bar but not appear on the menu bar. In other words, our menu bar will not display the CheckOut as the current page.

Our CheckOut is going to display the contents of the ShoppingCart to the customer but the way the items are displayed will be different to the way we displayed them on our Specials and Products Pages. This can been seen in our supermarket real world example. In a supermarket, items are displayed in orderly groups on supermarket shelves. At the checkout, the customer puts a jumble of items on the conveyor belt.

So, an item at checkout will need to be displayed slightly differently to an item on a Specials Page or a Products Page. For instance, we won't need to show the User an image of the item.

Also, we require different information about each item than we require on a Products or Specials Page.

Let's have a look at a CheckOut object;

```php
<?php
class CheckOut extends Page implements iPage{

    protected $title;
    protected $refresh;
    private $qs;
    private $cart;

    public function get_Title(){
        return $this->title;
    }
    public function get_Refresh(){
        return $this->refresh;
    }
    public function get_Cart(){
        return $this->cart;
    }

    public function __construct(){
        $this->title = MAIN_TITLE . CHECKOUT_TITLE;
        $this->refresh = false;
        $obj = new ObjectFactory();
        $this->cart = $obj->Create('ShoppingCart');
        parent::__construct();
```

```php
        }

        public function Initialise(){
                $this->qs = explode(QS_DELIMITER, $_SERVER['QUERY_STRING']);
                if(count($this->qs) > 1){
                        $this->cart->CheckItems($this->qs[0]);
                        if($this->qs[1] == 'RemoveItem' && is_Numeric($this->qs[0])){
                                $obj = new ObjectFactory();
                                $dba = $obj->Create('DbAdmin');
                                $dba->RemoveFromCart($this->qs[0], parent::get_User()-
>get_UserId());
                        }
                }else{
                        header('location: http://www.google.com');
                }
                return parent::Initialise();
        }

        public function writeContent(){
                $s = parent::writeHeading(SITE_HEADING . CHECKOUT_HEADING)
                        . $this->getMainContent();
                return $s;
        }

        private function getMainContent(){
                $s = '<div class="menu">' . parent::writeMenu() . '</div><div id="checkout">' .
                        CHECKOUT_SUB_HEADING . '<table summary="layout"><tr><td id="leftpane">';
                $obj = new ObjectFactory();
                if($this->qs[0] == 'PaymentWizard'){
                        $pw = $obj->Create('PaymentWizard');
                        $pw->set_UserId(parent::get_User()->get_UserId());
                        $s .= $pw->writeForm();
                }else{
                        $dba = $obj->Create('DbAdmin');
                        $rs = $dba->CartAtCheckout(parent::get_User()->get_UserId());
                        if(mysql_num_rows($rs) > 0){
                                $s .= '<h4>Cart Contents</h4><table summary="layout"
class="checkout"><tr><th>Item Purchased</th><th>Price</th><th>Remove Item</th></tr>';
                                for($i=0;$i<mysql_num_rows($rs);$i++){
                                        $row = mysql_fetch_row($rs);
                                        $itm = $obj->Create('ItemAtCheckout');
                                        $itm->set_Id($row[0]);
                                        $itm->set_ProductId($row[1]);
                                        $itm->set_Title($row[2]);
                                        $itm->set_Price($row[3]);
                                        $s .= $itm->DisplayRow();
                                }
                                $s .= '<tr><td></td><td><a href="' . SECURE_LNK . '?
PaymentWizard/CheckOut" class="proceed" title="Click to proceed to payment.">Make Payment
&gt;&gt;</a></td><td></td></tr></table>';
                        }else{
                                header('location: http://www.algyzone.com');
                        }
                }
                $s .= '</td><td id="rightpane"></td></tr></table>';
                return $s . '</div>';
        }

        public function Finalise(){
                return  parent::Finalise();
        }

        protected function onBeforeContent(){
                return '<div>Blah Blah Blah Blah Blah Blah Blah Blah Blah Blah Blah Blah Blah
</div>';
        }
```

```
    protected function onAfterContent(){
         return '<div>Blah Blah Blah Blah Blah Blah Blah Blah Blah Blah Blah Blah Blah
</div>';
    }

}
?>
```

The first line;

```
class CheckOut extends Page implements iPage{
```

tells us that we have a Page object. Nothing new here.

```
protected $title;
protected $refresh;
private $qs;
private $cart;

public function get_Title(){
     return $this->title;
}
public function get_Refresh(){
     return $this->refresh;
}
public function get_Cart(){
     return $this->cart;
}
```

Our Page properties are a little different though. Remember the Page object holds our User object and we can see that we have added a $cart object to our CheckOut object. So we have the three objects that model the real world. There is also a $qs property.

We move on to the constructor;

```
public function __construct(){
     $this->title = MAIN_TITLE . CHECKOUT_TITLE;
     $this->refresh = false;
     $obj = new ObjectFactory();
     $this->cart = $obj->Create('ShoppingCart');
     parent::__construct();
}
```

Here we see that we are asking the ObjectFactory to create a ShoppingCart object and asigning it ot our $cart property. So on instantion our CheckOut has all it's required objects in place.

Now we are going to initialise our Page object;

```
public function Initialise(){
```

```
        $this->qs = explode(QS_DELIMITER, $_SERVER['QUERY_STRING']);
        if(count($this->qs) > 1){
            $this->cart->CheckItems($this->qs[0]);
            if($this->qs[1] == 'RemoveItem' && is_Numeric($this-
>qs[0])){
                $obj = new ObjectFactory();
                $dba = $obj->Create('DbAdmin');
                $dba->RemoveFromCart($this->qs[0],
parent::get_User()->get_UserId());
            }
        }else{
            header('location: http://www.google.com');
        }
        return parent::Initialise();
    }
```

Here we explode our query string. `if(count($this->qs) > 1){` This line shows that we expect more than one parameter in our query string. If we don't have more than one parameter, it is likely that the User doesn't belong at the CheckOut and could be trying to hack us. So they get headered off to Google.

Next we ask the ShoppingCart to check it has items in it.

```
$this->cart->CheckItems($this->qs[0]);
```

The first item in the query string is the User Id. CheckItems actually makes the $cart property fill with items that are associated with the current User object.

The next block of code removes items from the shopping cart when the User clicks on a link we haven't seen yet.

So far we have built all our required objects and initialised our page.

Now we come down to the guts of it;

```
private function getMainContent(){
    $s = '<div id="checkout"><table summary="layout"><tr><td id="leftpane">';
    $obj = new ObjectFactory();
    if($this->qs[0] == 'PaymentWizard'){
        $pw = $obj->Create('PaymentWizard');
        $pw->set_UserId(parent::get_User()->get_UserId());
        $s .= $pw->writeForm();
    }else{
        $dba = $obj->Create('DbAdmin');
        $rs = $dba->CartAtCheckout(parent::get_User()->get_UserId());
        if(mysql_num_rows($rs) > 0){
            $s .= '<h4>Cart Contents</h4><table summary="layout"
class="checkout"><tr><th>Item Purchased</th><th>Price</th><th>Remove Item</th></tr>';
            for($i=0;$i<mysql_num_rows($rs);$i++){
                $row = mysql_fetch_row($rs);
                $itm = $obj->Create('ItemAtCheckout');
```

```
                                        $itm->set_Id($row[0]);
                                        $itm->set_ProductId($row[1]);
                                        $itm->set_Title($row[2]);
                                        $itm->set_Price($row[3]);
                                        $s .= $itm->DisplayRow();
                                }
                                $s .= '<tr><td></td><td><a href="' . SECURE_LNK . '?
PaymentWizard/CheckOut" class="proceed" title="Click to proceed to payment.">Make Payment
&gt;&gt;</a></td><td></td></tr></table>';
                        }else{
                                header('location: http://www.algyzone.com');
                        }
                }
        $s .= '</td><td id="rightpane"></td></tr></table>';
        return $s . '</div>';
}
```

This block of code;

```
$obj = new ObjectFactory();
if($this->qs[0] == 'PaymentWizard'){
        $pw = $obj->Create('PaymentWizard');
        $pw->set_UserId(parent::get_User()->get_UserId());
        $s .= $pw->writeForm();
}
```

Creates an ObjectFactory as we are going to need one. Then checks the query string to determine if the user has clicked the MakePayment >> link. If they have then the ObjectFactory creates a PaymentWizard and displays it.

If they haven't then the user is going to be removing items from their cart. This block of code runs;

```
else{
        $dba = $obj->Create('DbAdmin');
        $rs = $dba->CartAtCheckout(parent::get_User()->get_UserId());
        if(mysql_num_rows($rs) > 0){
                $s .= '<h4>Cart Contents</h4><table summary="layout"
class="checkout"><tr><th>Item Purchased</th><th>Price</th><th>Remove
Item</th></tr>';
                for($i=0;$i<mysql_num_rows($rs);$i++){
                        $row = mysql_fetch_row($rs);
                        $itm = $obj->Create('ItemAtCheckout');
                        $itm->set_Id($row[0]);
                        $itm->set_ProductId($row[1]);
                        $itm->set_Title($row[2]);
                        $itm->set_Price($row[3]);
                        $s .= $itm->DisplayRow();
                }
                $s .= '<tr><td></td><td><a href="' . SECURE_LNK . '?
PaymentWizard/CheckOut" class="proceed" title="Click to proceed to
payment.">Make Payment &gt;&gt;</a></td><td></td></tr></table>';
        }else{
```

```
        header('location: http://www.businessexample.com');
    }
```

We request a DbAdmin object and look at our cart at check out. If there are still items in the cart, we display them. If the cart is empty, we redirect the user to the landing page.

Our cart at check out currently looks like this;

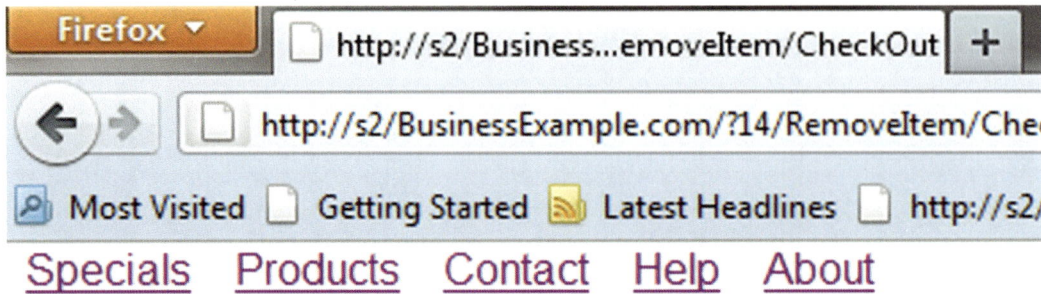

We'll click on the Make Payment >> link as we've already seen the landing page. This action will cause the first block of code to run and a PaymentWizard will be created. A PaymentWizard is a smart object and looks like this;

```php
<?php
class PaymentWizard{

    private $currentform = 1;
    private $uid;
    private $payment;

    public function set_UserId($val){ $this->uid = $val; }

    public function __construct(){

    }
```

```php
public function writeForm(){
        if(isset($_POST['submit'])){
                if($_POST['submit'] == 'Cancel'){
                        header('location: ' . DEFAULT_LNK);
                }
                if($_POST['submit'] == 'Next'){
                        $valid = true;
                        $obj = new ObjectFactory();
                        $v = $obj->Create('Validator');
                        if(!$v->isValid('cardname', addslashes($_POST['cardName']))){
                                $valid = false;
                        }
                        if(!$v->isValid('cardnumber', addslashes($_POST['cardNumber']))){
                                $valid = false;
                        }
                        if(!$v->isValid('ccv', addslashes($_POST['CCVNumber']))){
                                $valid = false;
                        }
                        if(!$v->isValid('email', addslashes($_POST['email']))){
                                $valid = false;
                        }
                        if($valid){
                                $this->currentform++;
                                $amt = $this->getPrice();
                                $p = $obj->Create('Payment');
                                if(addslashes($_POST['val']) == 'mast'){
                                        $p->set_CardType('MasterCard');
                                }else{
                                        $p->set_CardType('Visa');
                                }
                                $p->set_CardName(addslashes($_POST['cardName']));
                                $p->set_CardNumber(addslashes($_POST['cardNumber']));
                                $p->set_CCVNumber(addslashes($_POST['CCVNumber']));
                                $p->set_ExpMonth(addslashes($_POST['expmonth']));
                                $p->set_ExpYear(addslashes($_POST['expyear']));
                                $p->set_Amount($amt);
                                if(strlen($_POST['email']) > 5){
                                        $p->set_ReceiptAddress(addslashes($_POST['email']));
                                }
                                $p->StoreDetails();
                        }
                }
                if($_POST['submit'] == 'Make Payment'){
                        $this->currentform = 3;
                        $obj = new ObjectFactory();
                        $p = $obj->Create('Payment');
                        $this->payment = $p->RetrieveDetails();
                }
        }
        if($this->currentform != 3){
                $s = '<form id="paymentwizard" method="post"
action=""><fieldset><legend>Make Payment step ' . $this->currentform . ' of 3</legend>';
                $obj = new ObjectFactory();
                switch($this->currentform){
                        case 1:
                                $frm = $obj->Create('PaymentForm');
                                break;
                        case 2:
                                $frm = $obj->Create('ConfirmPaymentForm');
                                break;
                }
                if($this->currentform == 1){
                        $frm->set_Price($this->getPrice());
                }
                if($this->currentform == 1){
                        $s .= $frm->writeForm(true);
                }else{
```

```php
                                $s .= $frm->writeForm();
                        }
                        if($this->currentform == 2){
                                $s .= '<input type="submit" name="submit" value="Back" /> <input
type="submit" name="submit" value="Make Payment" />';
                        }else{
                                $s .= '<input type="submit" name="submit" value="Next" />';
                        }
                        $s .= ' <input type="submit" name="submit" value="Cancel"
/></fieldset></form>';
                }else{
                        $s = '<fieldset><legend>Make Payment step ' . $this->currentform . ' of
3</legend>';
                        if($this->payment->MakePayment()){
                                $s .= '<p>Payment Successful</p>';
                                $obj = new ObjectFactory();
                                $dba = $obj->Create('DbAdmin');
                                $dba->RecordPayment($this->uid);
                                $v = $obj->Create('Validator');
                                if($v->isValid('email', addslashes($this->payment-
>get_ReceiptAddress()))){
                                        if($this->payment->SendReceipt()){
                                                $s .= '<p>Receipt sent to ' . $this->payment-
>get_ReceiptAddress() . '</p>';
                                        }else{
                                                $s .= '<p>An error occurred sending the
receipt.</p>';
                                        }
                                }
                                $s .= '<p><a href="' . DEFAULT_LNK . '?' . DOWNLOAD_ACCESS .
'/Downloads" title="Proceed to Downloads." style="color: rgb(0, 0, 0); white-space:
nowrap;">Proceed to Downloads</a></p>';
                        }else{
                                $obj = new ObjectFactory();
                                $dba = $obj->Create('DbAdmin');
                                $dba->PurgeFromCart($this->uid);
                                $s .= '<p>Payment Unsuccessful <a href="' . DEFAULT_LNK . '"
title="Click to exit." style="color: rgb(0, 0, 0); white-space: nowrap;">Click to
exit.</a></p>';
                        }
                        $s .= '</fieldset>';
                }
                return $s;
        }

        private function getPrice(){
                $prc = 0.0;
                $obj = new ObjectFactory();
                $dba = $obj->Create('DbAdmin');
                $rs = $dba->CartAtCheckout($this->uid);
                if(mysql_num_rows($rs) > 0){
                        for($i=0;$i<mysql_num_rows($rs);$i++){
                                $row = mysql_fetch_row($rs);
                                $prc = $prc + $row[3];
                        }
                        $arr = explode('.', $prc);
                        if(strlen($arr[1]) == 1){
                                $prc = $arr[0] . '.' . $arr[1] . '0';
                        }
                }
                return $prc;
        }
}
?>
```

We start with the standard class definition `class PaymentWizard{` then define three private properties;

```php
private $currentform = 1;
private $uid;
private $payment;
```

The $currentform is set to 1 by default. We have a $uid and a $payment property. We have one accessor method;

```php
public function set_UserId($val){ $this->uid = $val; }
```

which set our $uid property to the current UserId. Then we have a constructor. All standard stuff that we have seen numerous times before.

We have just one public method called writeForm() that is common to all form objects. Most smart objects are forms of one sort or another.

```php
public function writeForm(){
    if(isset($_POST['submit'])){
        if($_POST['submit'] == 'Cancel'){
            header('location: ' . DEFAULT_LNK);
        }
```

First we look for a post back event. If the User has clicked the Cancel button, we redirect them to the landing page. We assume that they want to add more items to their cart.

At this point the user only has two choices. To cancel the payment or to proceed to the next step by clicking the Next button.

```php
if($_POST['submit'] == 'Next'){
    $valid = true;
    $obj = new ObjectFactory();
    $v = $obj->Create('Validator');
    if(!$v->isValid('cardname', addslashes($_POST['cardName']))){
        $valid = false;
    }
    if(!$v->isValid('cardnumber', addslashes($_POST['cardNumber']))){
        $valid = false;
    }
    if(!$v->isValid('ccv', addslashes($_POST['CCVNumber']))){
        $valid = false;
    }
    if(!$v->isValid('email', addslashes($_POST['email']))){
        $valid = false;
    }
    if($valid){
```

```
            $this->currentform++;
            $amt = $this->getPrice();
            $p = $obj->Create('Payment');
            if(addslashes($_POST['val']) == 'mast'){
                    $p->set_CardType('MasterCard');
            }else{
                    $p->set_CardType('Visa');
            }
            $p->set_CardName(addslashes($_POST['cardName']));
            $p->set_CardNumber(addslashes($_POST['cardNumber']));
            $p->set_CCVNumber(addslashes($_POST['CCVNumber']));
            $p->set_ExpMonth(addslashes($_POST['expmonth']));
            $p->set_ExpYear(addslashes($_POST['expyear']));
            $p->set_Amount($amt);
            if(strlen($_POST['email']) > 5){
                    $p->set_ReceiptAddress(addslashes($_POST['email']));
            }
            $p->StoreDetails();

    }
```

We check the post back event for the Next action. If we find it we have started the payment process. We create a variable called $valid and assign it the value of true. Then we request an ObjectFactory and create a Validator object.

```
$obj = new ObjectFactory();
    $v = $obj->Create('Validator');
    if(!$v->isValid('cardname', addslashes($_POST['cardName']))){
        $valid = false;
    }
    if(!$v->isValid('cardnumber', addslashes($_POST['cardNumber']))){
        $valid = false;
    }
    if(!$v->isValid('ccv', addslashes($_POST['CCVNumber']))){
        $valid = false;
    }
    if(!$v->isValid('email', addslashes($_POST['email']))){
        $valid = false;
    }
```

The block of code above asks the Validator to validate the user input from the payment form. If one input value is not valid, then we don't have a valid payment and the form will display error messages informing the User of the offending error.

If the User input is valid this block of code runs;

```
if($valid){
    $this->currentform++;
    $amt = $this->getPrice();
    $p = $obj->Create('Payment');
    if(addslashes($_POST['val']) == 'mast'){
```

```php
            $p->set_CardType('MasterCard');
        }else{
            $p->set_CardType('Visa');
        }
        $p->set_CardName(addslashes($_POST['cardName']));
        $p->set_CardNumber(addslashes($_POST['cardNumber']));
        $p->set_CCVNumber(addslashes($_POST['CCVNumber']));
        $p->set_ExpMonth(addslashes($_POST['expmonth']));
        $p->set_ExpYear(addslashes($_POST['expyear']));
        $p->set_Amount($amt);
        if(strlen($_POST['email']) > 5){
            $p->set_ReceiptAddress(addslashes($_POST['email']));
        }
        $p->StoreDetails();
    }
```

`$this->currentform++;` This line increments the current form from 1 to 2.

`$amt = $this->getPrice();` This line creates a local variable and calls a private function to get the amount that the transaction is going to be for.

This block of code;

```php
$p = $obj->Create('Payment');
if(addslashes($_POST['val']) == 'mast'){
    $p->set_CardType('MasterCard');
}else{
    $p->set_CardType('Visa');
}
$p->set_CardName(addslashes($_POST['cardName']));
$p->set_CardNumber(addslashes($_POST['cardNumber']));
$p->set_CCVNumber(addslashes($_POST['CCVNumber']));
$p->set_ExpMonth(addslashes($_POST['expmonth']));
$p->set_ExpYear(addslashes($_POST['expyear']));
$p->set_Amount($amt);
if(strlen($_POST['email']) > 5){
    $p->set_ReceiptAddress(addslashes($_POST['email']));
}
$p->StoreDetails();
```

creates a Payment object and assigns the validated input to several properties and then stores the payment details.

A Payment object looks like this;

```php
<?php
class Payment{

    private $_cardtype;
    private $_cardName;
    private $_cardNumber;
```

```php
    private $_CCVNumber;
    private $_expmonth;
    private $_expyear;
    private $_amount;
    private $_period;
    private $id;
    private $receiptnumber;
    private $receiptaddress;

    public function set_CardType($inct){$this->_cardtype = $inct;}
    public function get_CardType(){return $this->_cardtype;}
    public function set_CardName($incn){$this->_cardName = $incn;}
    public function get_CardName(){return $this->_cardName;}
    public function set_CardNumber($incm){$this->_cardNumber = $incm;}
    public function get_CardNumber(){return $this->_cardNumber;}
    public function set_CCVNumber($incc){$this->_CCVNumber = $incc;}
    public function get_CCVNumber(){return $this->_CCVNumber;}
    public function set_ExpMonth($inem){$this->_expmonth = $inem;}
    public function get_ExpMonth(){return $this->_expmonth;}
    public function set_ExpYear($iney){$this->_expyear = $iney;}
    public function get_ExpYear(){return $this->_expyear;}
    public function set_Amount($inamt){$this->_amount = $inamt;}
    public function get_Amount(){return $this->_amount;}
    public function set_Period($inamt){$this->_period = $inamt;}
    public function get_Period(){return $this->_period;}
    public function get_Id(){return $this->id;}
    public function get_ReceiptNumber(){return $this->receiptnumber;}
    public function get_ReceiptAddress(){return $this->receiptaddress;}
    public function set_ReceiptAddress($add){$this->receiptaddress = $add;}

    function __construct(){

    }

    public function StoreDetails(){
        $_SESSION['payment'] = serialize($this);
        return true;
    }

    public function RetrieveDetails(){
        return unserialize($_SESSION['payment']);
    }

    public function MakePayment(){
        $url = '';
        $ch = curl_init();
        curl_setopt($ch, CURLOPT_HEADER, false);
        curl_setopt($ch, CURLOPT_FOLLOWLOCATION, false);
        curl_setopt($ch, CURLOPT_SSL_VERIFYHOST,  false);
        curl_setopt($ch, CURLOPT_SSL_VERIFYPEER, false);
        curl_setopt($ch, CURLOPT_RETURNTRANSFER, true);
        curl_setopt($ch, CURLOPT_URL, $url);
        $result = curl_exec($ch);
        curl_close($ch);
        if(substr_count($result, 'status=approved') > 0){
            $this->receiptnumber = $this->getReceiptNumber($result);
            return true;
        }else{
            return false;
        }
        return false;
    }

    private function getReceiptNumber($result){
        $arr = explode('-----------------------', $result);
        $a = explode(' ', trim($arr[0]));
        return $a[count($a)-1];
```

```php
        }

        public function SendReceipt(){
                $obj = new ObjectFactory();
                $rec = $obj->Create('Receipt');
                $pst = $obj->Create('PostMaster');
                $pst->set_Address($this->get_ReceiptAddress());
                $pst->set_Subject('Receipt of purchase - Ducks and Dusters Pty Ltd');
                $pst->set_Message('Dear Sir/Madam<br /><br />Thank for purchasing software from
Ducks and Dusters Pty Ltd.<br /><br />Receipt details: <br />' . $rec->writeReceipt($this-
>get_ReceiptNumber(), $this->get_CardName(), $this->get_Amount()) . '<br /><br />Warm Regards<br
/>admin@ducksanddusters.com');
                $pst->set_From(RECEIPT_ADDRESS);
                return $pst->sendMail();
        }

        function Diagnose(){
                echo 'Card type = ' . $this->get_CardType() . '<br />';
                echo 'Card Name = ' . $this->get_CardName() . '<br />';
                echo 'Card Number = ' . $this->get_CardNumber() . '<br />';
                echo 'CCV Number = ' . $this->get_CCVNumber() . '<br />';
                echo 'Exp Month = ' . $this->get_ExpMonth() . '<br />';
                echo 'Exp Year = ' . $this->get_ExpYear() . '<br />';
                echo 'Amount = ' . $this->get_Amount() . '<br />';
        }

}
?>
```

Another smart object. We see a set of properties and their accessor functions above the constructor.

Below the constructor we see two public methods;

```php
public function StoreDetails(){
        $_SESSION['payment'] = serialize($this);
        return true;
}

public function RetrieveDetails(){
        return unserialize($_SESSION['payment']);
}
```

These are used to store and retrieve the payment object in a session valiable. This is a safe way of storing the payment as we are using a SSL link to make the transaction. That means we will return, on post back, to the same server and therefore the same session. We don't want to store credit card details in our database.

The public method

```php
public function MakePayment(){
        $url = '';
        $ch = curl_init();
        curl_setopt($ch, CURLOPT_HEADER, false);
        curl_setopt($ch, CURLOPT_FOLLOWLOCATION, false);
```

```
curl_setopt($ch, CURLOPT_SSL_VERIFYHOST,  false);
curl_setopt($ch, CURLOPT_SSL_VERIFYPEER, false);
curl_setopt($ch, CURLOPT_RETURNTRANSFER, true);
curl_setopt($ch, CURLOPT_URL, $url);
$result = curl_exec($ch);
curl_close($ch);
if(substr_count($result, 'status=approved') > 0){
        $this->receiptnumber = $this->getReceiptNumber($result);
        return true;
}else{
        return false;
}
return false;
}
```

Makes the payment transaction using an asynchronous connection to the payment gateway. On a successful payment, it retrieves the receipt number from the returned value.

This public method

```
public function SendReceipt(){
        $obj = new ObjectFactory();
        $rec = $obj->Create('Receipt');
        $pst = $obj->Create('PostMaster');
        $pst->set_Address($this->get_ReceiptAddress());
        $pst->set_Subject('Receipt of purchase - Ducks and Dusters Pty
Ltd');
        $pst->set_Message('Dear Sir/Madam<br /><br />Thank for purchasing
software from Ducks and Dusters Pty Ltd.<br /><br />Receipt details: <br />'
. $rec->writeReceipt($this->get_ReceiptNumber(), $this->get_CardName(),
$this->get_Amount()) . '<br /><br />Warm Regards<br
/>admin@ducksanddusters.com');
        $pst->set_From(RECEIPT_ADDRESS);
        return $pst->sendMail();
}
```

Sends a receipt to the customer. Back to the Payment Wizard....

This block of code;

```
if($_POST['submit'] == 'Make Payment'){
        $this->currentform = 3;
        $obj = new ObjectFactory();
        $p = $obj->Create('Payment');
        $this->payment = $p->RetrieveDetails();
}
```

Recognises the last step of the payment process and grabs the payment object out of session.

The next block of code is looking for movement within the wizard.

```php
if($this->currentform != 3){
        $s = '<form id="paymentwizard" method="post"
action=""><fieldset><legend>Make Payment step ' . $this->currentform . ' of
3</legend>';
        $obj = new ObjectFactory();
        switch($this->currentform){
            case 1:
                    $frm = $obj->Create('PaymentForm');
                    break;
            case 2:
                    $frm = $obj->Create('ConfirmPaymentForm');
                    break;
        }
        if($this->currentform == 1){
                $frm->set_Price($this->getPrice());
        }
        if($this->currentform == 1){
                $s .= $frm->writeForm(true);
        }else{
                $s .= $frm->writeForm();
        }
        if($this->currentform == 2){
                $s .= '<input type="submit" name="submit" value="Back" />
<input type="submit" name="submit" value="Make Payment" />';
        }else{
                $s .= '<input type="submit" name="submit" value="Next" />';
        }
        $s .= ' <input type="submit" name="submit" value="Cancel"
/></fieldset></form>';
    }
```

So it determines that we are not at step 3 in the process and decides what form to present to the user. The ConfirmPaymentForm will present the user input with the credit card number XXXed out. It only contains properties.

If we are up to step 3 in the payment process, the next block of code;

```php
else{
        $s = '<fieldset><legend>Make Payment step ' . $this-
>currentform . ' of 3</legend>';
        if($this->payment->MakePayment()){
                $s .= '<p>Payment Successful</p>';
                $obj = new ObjectFactory();
                $dba = $obj->Create('DbAdmin');
                $dba->RecordPayment($this->uid);
                $v = $obj->Create('Validator');
                if($v->isValid('email', addslashes($this->payment-
```

```php
>get_ReceiptAddress()))){
                        if($this->payment->SendReceipt()){
                                $s .= '<p>Receipt sent to ' . $this->payment-
>get_ReceiptAddress() . '</p>';
                        }else{
                                $s .= '<p>An error occurred sending the
receipt.</p>';
                        }
                }
                $s .= '<p><a href="' . DEFAULT_LNK . '?DeliveryDetails"
title="Proceed to Delivery Details." style="color: rgb(0, 0, 0); white-space:
nowrap;">Proceed to Delivery Details</a></p>';
        }else{
                $obj = new ObjectFactory();
                $dba = $obj->Create('DbAdmin');
                $dba->PurgeFromCart($this->uid);
                $s .= '<p>Payment Unsuccessful <a href="' . DEFAULT_LNK .
'" title="Click to exit." style="color: rgb(0, 0, 0); white-space:
nowrap;">Click to exit.</a></p>';
        }
        $s .= '</fieldset>';
}
```

Exercises the Payment object seen above. On a successful payment we give the User a link to a DeliveryDetails Page object. This differs from most design models that take delivery details before making the payment. I have opted to do it this way as I have taken the payment and at the same time validated my User as a legitimate customer. The User has made the payment and now has a vested interest in receiving their goods. There is a very good chance that they are going to enter in all the details I want from them for my marketing campaign.

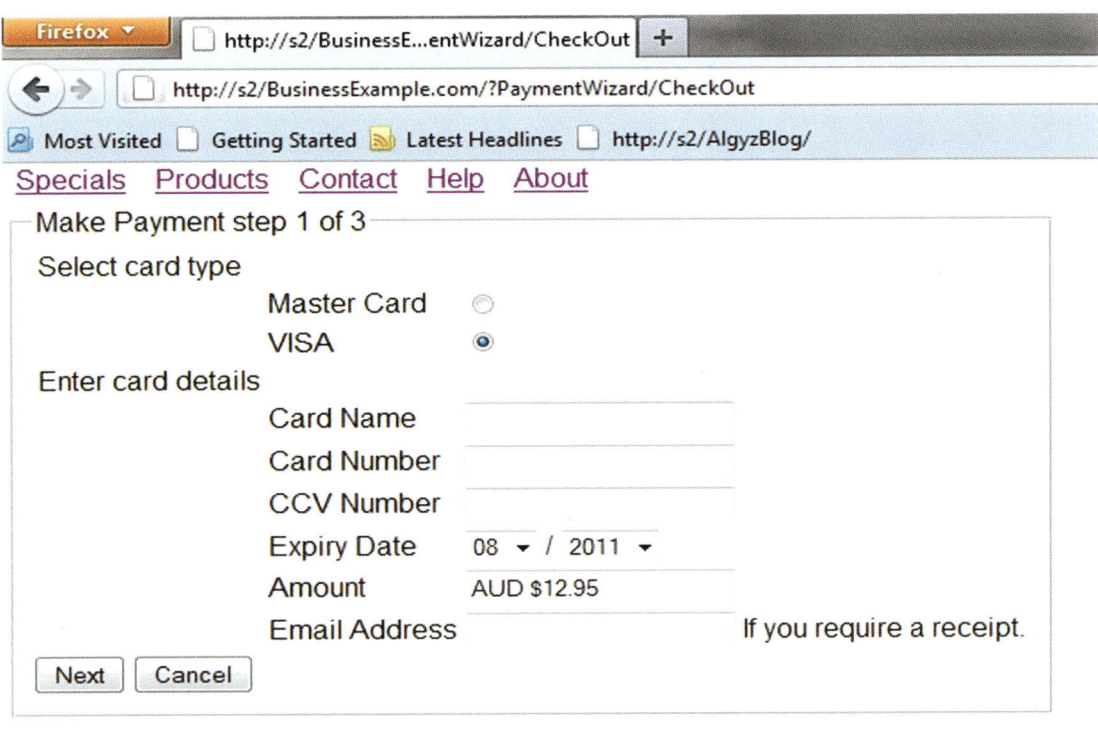

Firefox ▾ | http://s2/BusinessE...entWizard/CheckOut | +

← → http://s2/BusinessExample.com/?PaymentWizard/CheckOut

🔎 Most Visited ☐ Getting Started 📰 Latest Headlines ☐ http://s2/AlgyzBlog/

Specials   Products   Contact   Help   About

Make Payment step 1 of 3

Select card type

Master Card	○
VISA	●

Enter card details

Card Name

Card Number

CCV Number

Expiry Date   08 ▾ / 2011 ▾

Amount   AUD $12.95

Email Address   If you require a receipt.

[Next] [Cancel]

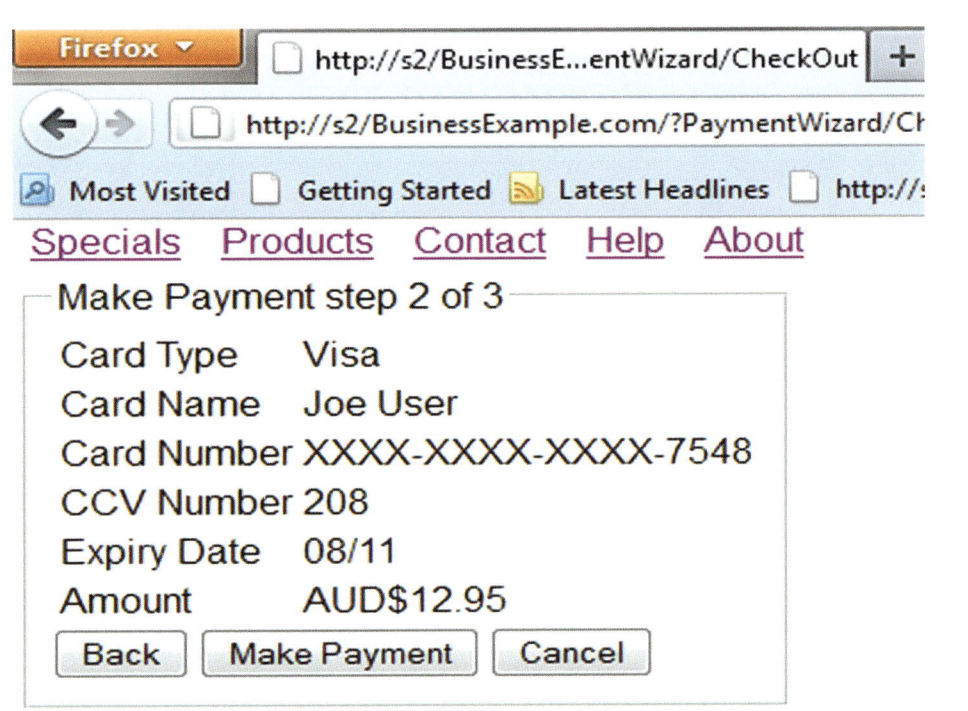

Firefox ▾ | http://s2/BusinessE...entWizard/CheckOut | +

← → http://s2/BusinessExample.com/?PaymentWizard/Ch

🔎 Most Visited ☐ Getting Started 📰 Latest Headlines ☐ http://s

Specials   Products   Contact   Help   About

Make Payment step 2 of 3

Card Type   Visa
Card Name   Joe User
Card Number   XXXX-XXXX-XXXX-7548
CCV Number   208
Expiry Date   08/11
Amount   AUD$12.95

[Back] [Make Payment] [Cancel]

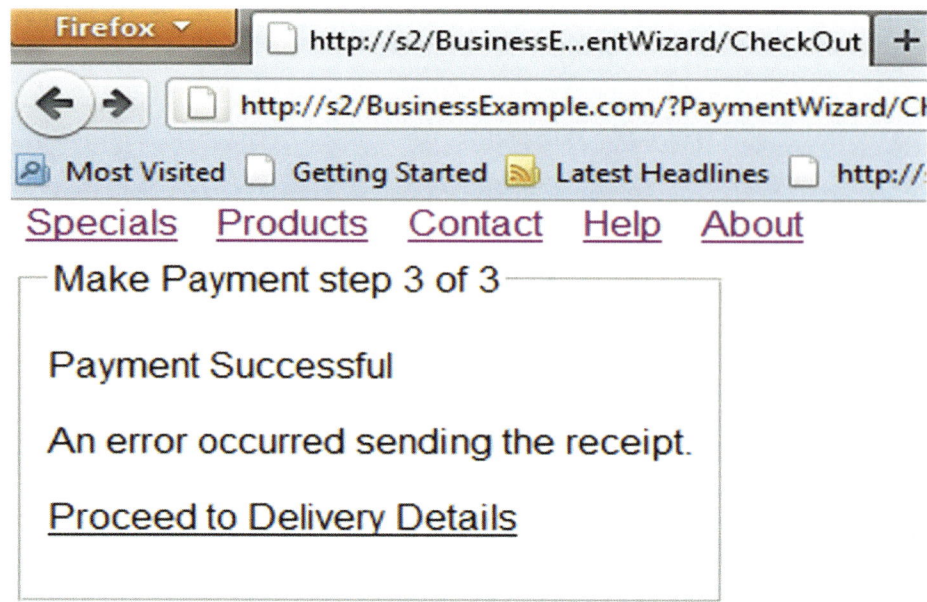

Above are images of the three steps of the payment wizard just to prove that the code works.

The error occurred sending the receipt because I don't have an SMTP server setup in my development environment for security reasons.

The DeliveryDetails Page object looks like this;

```php
<?php
class DeliveryDetails extends Page implements iPage{

    protected $title;
    protected $refresh;

    public function get_Title(){
        return $this->title;
    }
    public function get_Refresh(){
        return $this->refresh;
    }

    public function __construct(){
        $this->title = INDEX_TITLE;
        $this->refresh = false;
        parent::__construct();
    }
```

```php
        public function Initialise(){
                return parent::Initialise();
        }

        public function writeContent(){
                return parent::writeMenu() . '<h3>Delivery Details</h3>' . $this-
>getMainContent();
        }

        private function getMainContent(){
                $obj = new ObjectFactory();
                $frm = $obj->Create('RegistrationForm');
                $frm->set_Fields(Array('email', 'fname', 'lname', 'address1', 'address2',
'postcode', 'phone', 'mobile', 'state', 'country'));
                $frm->set_ReqFields(Array('email', 'fname', 'lname', 'address1', 'address2',
'postcode', 'state', 'country'));
                return $frm->writeForm();
        }

        public function Finalise(){
                return  parent::Finalise();
        }

        protected function onBeforeContent(){
                return '<div>Blah Blah Blah Blah Blah Blah Blah Blah Blah Blah Blah Blah Blah
</div>';
        }

        protected function onAfterContent(){
                return '<div>Blah Blah Blah Blah Blah Blah Blah Blah Blah Blah Blah Blah Blah
</div>';
        }

}
?>
```

So the standard Page Type objects we've seen before. The main point to note is that I am instantiating a RegistrationForm smart object that is a generic registration form I developed some time ago. It takes two arrays of field names that will be displayed on the form. The first array entered into the $frm->set_Fields() property is a list of all the fields that will be displayed on the form. The second array entered into the $frm->set_ReqFields() property is a list of all the required fields that will then be validated on form input.

The RegistrationForm object looks like this;

```php
<?php
class RegistrationForm{

        protected $err;
        protected $fields;
        protected $reqfields;

        //possible fields'email', 'pwd', 'confirm', 'humid', 'fname', 'lname', 'address1',
'address2', 'postcode', 'phone', 'mobile','workphone', 'fax', 'state', 'country', 'timezone'
        public function set_Fields($fld){
                $this->fields = $fld;
        }
        public function set_ReqFields($qfld){
                $this->reqfields = $qfld;
        }
```

```php
public function __construct(){
        $this->err['email'] = false;
        $this->err['pwd'] = false;
        $this->err['confirm'] = false;
        $this->err['humid'] = false;
        $this->err['fname'] = false;
        $this->err['lname'] = false;
        $this->err['address1'] = false;
        $this->err['address2'] = false;
        $this->err['phone'] = false;
        $this->err['mobile'] = false;
        $this->err['fax'] = false;
        $this->err['state'] = false;
        $this->err['country'] = false;
        $this->err['timezone'] = false;
        $this->err['postcode'] = false;
        $this->err['workphone'] = false;
        $this->err['notright'] = false;
        $this->err['dupuser'] = false;
        if(isset($_POST['submit'])){
            if(addslashes($_POST['submit']) == 'Register'){
                $obj = new ObjectFactory();
                $v = $obj->Create('Validator');
                if(isset($_POST['email'])){
                    if(!$v->isValid('email', addslashes($_POST['email']))){
                        $this->err['email'] = true;
                    }
                }
                if(!$v->isValid('dupe', addslashes($_POST['email']))){
                    $this->err['dupuser'] = true;
                }
                if(isset($_POST['pwd'])){
                    if(!$v->isValid('pwd', addslashes($_POST['pwd']))){
                        $this->err['pwd'] = true;
                    }
                }
                if(isset($_POST['confirm'])){
                    $arr[0] = addslashes($_POST['pwd']);
                    $arr[1] = addslashes($_POST['confirm']);
                    if(!$v->isValid('confirm', $arr)){
                        $this->err['confirm'] = true;
                    }
                }
                if(isset($_POST['fname'])){
                    if(!$v->isValid('fname', addslashes($_POST['fname']))){
                        $this->err['fname'] = true;
                    }
                    if(!$v->isValid('lname', addslashes($_POST['lname']))){
                        $this->err['lname'] = true;
                    }
                }
                if(isset($_POST['address1'])){
                    if(!$v->isValid('address1',
addslashes($_POST['address1']))){
                        $this->err['address1'] = true;
                    }
                    if(!$v->isValid('address2',
addslashes($_POST['address2']))){
                        $this->err['address2'] = true;
                    }
                }
                if(isset($_POST['phone'])){
                    if(!$v->isValid('phone', addslashes($_POST['phone']))){
                        $this->err['phone'] = true;
                    }
                }
                if(isset($_POST['mobile'])){
```

```php
                    if(!$v->isValid('mobile', addslashes($_POST['mobile']))){
                        $this->err['mobile'] = true;
                    }
                }
                if(isset($_POST['workphone'])){
                    if(!$v->isValid('phone', addslashes($_POST['workphone']))){
                        $this->err['workphone'] = true;
                    }
                }
                if(isset($_POST['humid'])){
                    if($v->isValid('humid', addslashes($_POST['humid']))){
                        switch(addslashes($_POST['hid'])){
                            case '1':
                                if(addslashes($_POST['humid']) !=
'NW5k'){
                                    $this->err['notright'] = true;
                                }
                            break;
                            case '2':
                                if(addslashes($_POST['humid']) !=
'Q2#C'){
                                    $this->err['notright'] = true;
                                }
                            break;
                            case '3':
                                if(addslashes($_POST['humid']) !=
'H8G&'){
                                    $this->err['notright'] = true;
                                }
                            break;
                            case '4':
                                if(addslashes($_POST['humid']) != 'Z
%A9'){
                                    $this->err['notright'] = true;
                                }
                            break;
                        }
                    }else{
                        $this->err['humid'] = true;
                    }
                }
                if(isset($_POST['fax'])){
                    if(!$v->isValid('fax', addslashes($_POST['fax']))){
                        $this->err['fax'] = true;
                    }
                }
                if(isset($_POST['state'])){
                    if(!$v->isValid('state', addslashes($_POST['state']))){
                        $this->err['state'] = true;
                    }
                }
                if(isset($_POST['country'])){
                    if(!$v->isValid('country', addslashes($_POST['country']))){
                        $this->err['country'] = true;
                    }
                }
                if(isset($_POST['timezone'])){
                    if(!$v->isValid('timezone',
addslashes($_POST['timezone']))){
                        $this->err['timezone'] = true;
                    }
                }
                if(isset($_POST['postcode'])){
                    if(!$v->isValid('postcode',
addslashes($_POST['postcode']))){
                        $this->err['postcode'] = true;
                    }
```

```php
					}
				}
			}
		}

	public function writeForm($file = false, $pay = false, $secure = false){
		$arr = $this->fields;
		$s = '<form name="register" id="register" method="post"';
		if($file){
			$s .= ' enctype="multipart/form-data"';
		}
		if($secure){
			$s .= ' action="' . HTTPS . '"';
		}
		$s .= '><table summary="layout">';
		for($i=0;$i<count($arr);$i++){
			if(isset($_POST[$arr[$i]])){
				if($arr[$i] == 'humid'){
					$s .= $this->getHumid();
				}else{
					$s .= '<tr><td class="label">' . $this->getLabel($arr[$i]);
					if(in_array($arr[$i], $this->reqfields)){
						$s .= '<span class="req">*</span>';
					}
					$s .= '</label></td>
					<td><input' . $this->Attributes($arr[$i]) . ' name="' .
$arr[$i] . '" value="' . addslashes(stripslashes($_POST[$arr[$i]])) . '" /></td>
					<td class="error">';
					if($this->err[$arr[$i]]){
						if(in_array($arr[$i], $this->reqfields)){
							$s .= 'This is a required field.';
						}
					}else if($arr[$i] == 'email'){
						if($this->err['dupuser']){
							$s .= 'Email already registered. Have you
forgotten your password?';
						}
					}else if($arr[$i] == 'confirm'){
						if($this->err['confirm']){
							$s .= 'Password and Confirm must match.';
						}
					}
					$s .= '</td></tr>';
				}
			}else{
				if($arr[$i] == 'humid'){
					$s .= $this->getHumid();
				}else{
					$s .= '<tr><td class="label">' . $this->getLabel($arr[$i]);
					if(in_array($arr[$i], $this->reqfields)){
						$s .= '<span class="req">*</span>';
					}
					$s .= '</label></td>
					<td><input' . $this->Attributes($arr[$i]) . ' name="' .
$arr[$i] . '" /></td><td class="error">';
					if($this->err[$arr[$i]]){
						if(in_array($arr[$i], $this->reqfields)){
							$s .= 'This is a required field.';
						}
					}
					$s .= '</td></tr>';
				}
			}
		}
		if($pay){
			$s .= '<tr><td>Permanent Account</td><td><input type="checkbox"
name="paid" /></td><td></td></tr>';
```

```php
            }
            $s .= '<tr><td></td><td><input type="submit" name="submit" value="Register"
/></td><td></td></tr>';
            $s .= '</table></form>';
            return $s;
        }

    private function getHumid(){
            $w = $this->scrambleMe();
            $s = '<tr><td><label for="humid">Human Id<span
class="req">*</span></label></td><td>';
            $s .= '<input type="text" name="humid" value="' . $w['value'] . '"
maxlength="4" /></td><td>';
            if($this->err['notright']){
                    $s .= '<span class="error">Human Id and input don\'t match.</span>';
                    }
            if($this->err['humid']){
                    $s .= '<span class="error">This is a required field.</span>';
                    }
            $s .= '</td></tr><tr><td></td><td>';
            $s .= '<img src="' . $w['img'] . '" name="' . $w['name'] . '" id="uhid1"
onclick="swap(this);" /><input type="hidden" name="hid" value="' . $w['hid'] . '" size="1"
maxlength="1" /></td></tr></tr>';
            $s .= '<tr><td colspan="3"><span style="font-size: x-small;">Enter the characters
in the space provided. If unsure, click on the characters to swap.</span></td></tr>';
            return $s;
        }

    private function scrambleMe(){
            $i = rand(1, 4);
            $arr = Array();
            $arr['img'] = 'Images/Reg/uid' . $i . '.jpg';
            $arr['name'] = 'uhid' . $i;
            $arr['value'] = '';
            $arr['hid'] = $i;
            return $arr;
        }

    private function Attributes($at){
            $a = '';
            switch(strtolower($at)){
                    case 'pwd':
                    case 'confirm':
                            $a = ' type="password"';
                    break;
                    case 'state':
                    case 'country':
                    case 'timezone':
                            $a = '';
                    break;
                    default:
                            $a = ' type="text"';
                    break;
            }
            return $a;
        }

    private function getLabel($str){
            $n = '';
            switch(strtolower($str)){
            case 'email':
                $n = 'Email';
            break;
            case 'pwd':
                $n = 'Password';
            break;
            case 'confirm':
```

```php
                $n = 'Confirm Pwd';
        break;
        case 'humid':
                $n = 'Human Id';
        break;
        case 'fname':
                $n = 'First Name';
        break;
        case 'lname':
                $n = 'Last Name';
        break;
        case 'address1':
                $n = 'Address 1';
        break;
        case 'address2':
                $n = 'Address 2';
        break;
        case 'phone':
                $n = 'Phone';
        break;
        case 'mobile':
                $n = 'Mobile';
        break;
        case 'fax':
                $n = 'Fax';
        break;
        case 'state':
                $n = 'State';
        break;
        case 'country':
                $n = 'Country';
        break;
        case 'timezone':
                $n = 'Time Zone';
        break;
        case 'postcode':
                $n = 'Post Code';
        break;
        case 'workphone':
                $n = 'Work Phone';
        break;
        }
        return $n;
    }

}
?>
```

It looks more complicated than it really is. It basically takes the first array and builds all the labels and input boxes and then validates the input against the second array. It has an outdated antispam device that I have replaced in newer versions with an object that builds graphics on the fly and ships with the framework that can be downloaded using the link at the end of the book.

The registration form looks like this;

Specials   Products   Contact   Help   About

Delivery Details

Email*

First Name*

Last Name*

Address 1*

Address 2*

Post Code*

Phone

Mobile

State*

Country*

[Register]

And validation looks like;

Delivery Details

Email*		This is a required field.
First Name*		This is a required field.
Last Name*		This is a required field.
Address 1*		This is a required field.
Address 2*		This is a required field.
Post Code*		This is a required field.
Phone		
Mobile		
State*		This is a required field.
Country*		This is a required field.

Register

It has taken about 55 minutes to build the site in this example. Admittedly there is still a lot more work to go. But all the work is simply applying CSS style sheets to the pages to make them presentable on the web. All the functionality that a commercial website requires has been implemented. All the objects have been tested previously and this site will function without errors.

If your time frame for the project is 3 months, then you have nearly the entire time to play with CSS styles.

To download the Framework, follow this link;

http://www.algyzone.com/?7e4127016040d72fcce0176a027f12d3/FrameworkDownload

and enter this code in the space provided;

`FOIHS84Z`

Please use the contact form at http://www.algyzone.com/?Contact if you require further information.

I hope you have as much fun using the Framework as I do!

CPSIA information can be obtained
at www.ICGtesting.com
Printed in the USA
LVIW020802290513
335930LV00005B